Praise for *The Pregnancy B*

"Amy E. Tracy writes from experience, having survived many weeks of bed rest during her own high-risk pregnancies. Her practical and comprehensive guide provides an expectant mother with everything she needs to follow doctor's orders and help ensure the birth of a full-term, healthy baby. It's the perfect bedside companion."

　　—Carol Cirulli Lanham, author of *Pregnancy After a Loss*

"*The Pregnancy Bed Rest Book* is an excellent compilation of coping tips from real-life families on how to survive a complicated pregnancy. [It also offers] great lists of resources of all kinds right at your fingertips. This is a necessary book for any expectant mother who may spend four days or four months in bed."

　　—Tracy Hoogenboom, director, Sidelines National Support Network

"Long awaited and much needed, this book is packed with practical pointers and encouraging stories from mothers who survived bed rest stints at home and in the hospital. . . . This indispensable book offers immediate relief from the restlessness of bed rest."

　　—Sharon Withers, managing editor, *TWINS Magazine*

continued . . .

"Supportive, hopeful, well researched, and written in a clear, friendly style, Amy E. Tracy's new book is a practical, essential guide.... [It is] sure to become a cherished companion for many expectant mothers. Ms. Tracy covers everything you need to know to stay healthy while horizontal, from prioritizing to planning, work to washing, eating to intimacy, and muscle tone to mental health. Everything I wish I'd known during my own bout with bed rest—and more!"

—Elizabeth A. Pector, M.D., F.A.A.P., family physician and bed rest veteran

"Bed rest is one of the most difficult therapies we can ask of a woman and her family.... *The Pregnancy Bed Rest Book* is a gift to those in this circumstance. Within are the tools and wisdom of experience to take on bed rest as an opportunity and creative process and as a time of personal and family growth. *The Pregnancy Bed Rest Book* will help you remain connected to all that matters."

—Robert N. Wolfson, M.D., Ph.D., perinatologist and president of Specialists in Women's Health, Colorado Springs, Colorado

Praise for *Your Premature Baby and Child*

"Parents will find comfort in these pages and a helpful commonsense guide to the challenges of life with a premature baby."

> —Anne Casey, mother of a premature infant and founder of the Internet support group Preemie-L

"*Your Premature Baby and Child* educates, encourages, and empowers parents. I will recommend this book to parents and professionals alike."

> —Sandra Gardner, R.N., M.S., C.N.S., P.N.P., coeditor of *The Handbook of Neonatal Intensive Care*

"As a comprehensive reference, this book is an invaluable tool for bridging the communication gap between the healthcare provider and parent."

> —James Boehlke, M.D., F.A.A.P., pediatrician and father of preterm twin daughters

"This book continues the story of caring for your premature baby from the point where other books stop."

> —Allison Martin, founder of the Internet resource Premature Child

"Each section of the book gives a good mixture of accurate medical information, true-life experiences, and practical advice for parents. I think it is the best preemie resource available today."

> —Cynthia Bissell, mother of preemie twins

The Pregnancy Bed Rest Book

*A Survival Guide for Expectant
Mothers and Their Families*

AMY E. TRACY

Foreword by
Richard H. Schwarz, M.D.,
obstetrical consultant, March of Dimes

B

BERKLEY BOOKS, NEW YORK

B

A Berkley Book
Published by The Berkley Publishing Group
A division of Penguin Putnam Inc.
375 Hudson Street
New York, New York 10014

Kind permission was granted to use the following:
Pages 75 and 82: Food source and serving-size guide and A Healthy Sample Menu provided by March of Dimes, 1275 Mamaroneck Ave., White Plains, NY 10605.
Page 93: Baby Pick-Me-Up: A High-Energy Drink, reprinted from *Eating Expectantly* by Bridget Swinney, M.S., R.N. (Meadowbrook Press, 2000) © 2000 by Bridget Swinney.
Page 168: Bed Rest's Silver Lining by Lauri Krauth, M.A., L.L.P. © 2000 by Lauri Krauth.

PRINTING HISTORY
Berkley trade paperback edition / October 2001

Visit our website at
www.penguinputnam.com

Library of Congress Cataloging-in-Publication Data

Tracy, Amy E.
The pregnancy bed rest book : a survival guide for expectant mothers and their families
/ Amy E. Tracy ; foreword by Richard H. Schwarz.
p.   cm.
ISBN 0-425-18166-9
I. Pregnancy.   2. Pregnancy—Complications—Prevention.   3. Bed rest.   I. Title.

RG572 .T73 2001
618.2'4—dc21

2001035371

PRINTED IN THE UNITED STATES OF AMERICA

10   9   8   7   6   5   4   3   2   1

For the children

*The flower that blooms in the face of adversity
is the most beautiful flower of all.*

—Unknown

CONTENTS

Contents

When I was invited by Amy Tracy to write a foreword for this book, my response, before reading the text, was: How could there be enough material on the subject of bed rest to fill a book? I suspect many obstetricians might have reacted the same way, despite the fact that they often prescribe bed rest for their patients.

Bed rest is recommended for a number of pregnancy complications, and statistics estimate that as many as one in five pregnant women receive such a prescription. Some physicians consider the use of bed rest controversial, as there are not a lot of controlled studies to prove its effectiveness; nonetheless, every obstetrician I know does recommend bed rest as part of treatment for at least some pregnancy complications.

How bed rest helps is not clear in every case. The horizontal position does increase blood flow to the kidneys and the uterus, and also reduces gravity-forced pressure on the cervix. Energy is conserved with inactivity, hopefully producing a more favorable nutritional balance toward the fetus. Equally important, the prescription of bed rest gives the patient and her family the sense that everything possible is being done to avoid a pregnancy loss. Should a loss occur despite all efforts, that sense may help to reduce feelings of guilt.

As with most obstetricians who recommend bed rest to a pregnant woman with a complication, I know I have not always thoroughly appreciated, or counseled a patient about, the full impact of that prescription on her and her family. Having been there herself and having gathered information from a large number of other women who have survived bed rest, Ms. Tracy has compiled not only a comprehensive description of the problems, but an equally complete set of recommendations for dealing with them.

Often the pregnancy complication and the need for bed rest arise suddenly and unexpectedly, causing the woman and her family to face myriad problems, some of which they may not even be aware of. This book can be an invaluable resource under such circumstances. Even when the bed-rest decision is anticipated, Ms. Tracy's book will be helpful in anticipating and preparing for the problems ahead.

Beyond the actual text, the listings of resources, including reading material, Web sites, and support group information, are not likely to be easily found elsewhere. It would probably be worthwhile for obstetricians, and especially for perinatologists, to have a copy or two available in the office to lend to the woman who has just been told to "get off her feet"—until she can get a copy of her own.

—Richard H. Schwarz, M.D.,
    obstetrical consultant to March of Dimes Birth Defects Foundation and past president of the American College of Obstetricians and Gynecologists

SOME PRACTICAL NOTES

If you bought or were given this book soon after at-home bed rest was prescribed, or you're anticipating a bed-rest pregnancy, you'll probably want to start reading from page one. Even if you've been on bed rest for a few weeks and just opened up the book, the early sections and chapters can be helpful. However, chapters do not need to be read consecutively. For instance, if you begin bed rest in the hospital, you may first want to read chapter 4, When Hospitalization Is Needed.

While this book is not meant to offer medical advice, I believe it is crucial for a woman facing a high-risk pregnancy to empower herself with information. To complement the information your doctor provides, I have included medical-related books, organizations, and Web sites in chapter 1 and appendix D.

One of my frustrations during bed rest was not having a central resource to go to for answers. That's why I created Who Can Help and Recommended Reading at the end of most chapters; these are resources specific to chapter topics. Other resources pertaining to complicated pregnancies and bed rest, as well as some topics not specifically addressed in the book, are offered in appendix D.

To facilitate readability and because most readers will be pregnant women (single or married), I primarily refer to the reader as the expectant mother. However, I hope many expectant fathers and partners will read this book, too (in some places, I refer to fathers, but do not mean to exclude same-sex partners). I also refer to all babies in the singular, unless information is specific to multiple gestations (however, I expect many readers will be carrying multiple babies).

I have tried to represent fairly all types of families in my writing, and used a wide psychosocial and geographic representation in my research. To protect their privacy, names and any identifying characteristics of parents have been changed.

Finally, I would love to hear from you. If you'd like to share your story, chat with other bed-resting moms-to-be, or comment on the book, visit my Web site at www.pregnancybedrest.com, or write to me at 445C E. Cheyenne Mountain Blvd., P.M.B. 194, Colorado Springs, CO 80906.

ACKNOWLEDGMENTS

One of the greatest rewards of writing this book has been meeting so many warm, giving people and receiving so much kindness and support. I hope that each of you will feel as though this is your book, and that you will take pride in knowing your generosity is helping many women and their families facing bed rest.

Special gratitude goes to the following people: First and foremost, to the Bed Rest Book Buddies: Cindy Belsky, A. Maureen Corbett-Gentile, Kelly Feevey, Jennifer Gillett, Andrea Gordon, Christi Hayes, Jan Page, Linda Reichert, and Delia Higgs Weikert. Also to the many families who let me step into their lives. Thank you for sharing your time, your personal experiences, and your wisdom. This book could not have been written without you.

To Judith A. Maloni, Ph.D., R.N., who was there from start to finish, unselfishly giving her valuable research, expertise, and guidance. I hope this book assists you in the wonderful work you do.

To Laurie Krauth, M.A., L.L.P., Deborah S. Simmons, Ph.D., and

Mara Stein, Psy.D., for reviewing the various sections and chapters dealing with emotional issues and answering all those E-mails.

To Bridget Swinney, M.S., R.D., for reviewing chapter 5, as well as for your encouragement, support, and friendship over the years.

To Cora Huitt, P.T., M.A., and Elizabeth Noble, P.T., for their reviews of chapters 6 and 10; to Jeanne Pinnon, human resources expert, for reviewing chapter 2; and to Beth Mosele, social worker, for reviewing chapters 2 and 4. Thank you.

To Christine Zika and the folks at Berkley for recognizing the need for this book.

My heartfelt appreciation also goes to Jane Chelius, literary agent extraordinaire. Thank you for helping to make my dreams come true.

And finally, to my family, far and near; to my husband, George; to my sons, Daniel Edward and Steven James; and to the baby I never knew. I love you all.

INTRODUCTION

Where there is great love there are always miracles.

⌒ Willa Cather

Nearly eleven years ago and during my eighteenth week of pregnancy, my obstetrician prescribed bed rest for unexplained bleeding. Having lost my first baby, I was more than willing to put my life on hold if it even slightly increased my chances of having a healthy baby. But as good as my intentions were, I soon learned that lying low was not nearly as easy as it sounded.

I hated feeling like I had no control over my life, and I didn't like relying on others to take care of my family, my home, my work, and me. I felt angry, frustrated, and sad.

Not wanting to further burden those who were helping me, I began writing down my thoughts in a red spiral-bound notebook. As the days passed, I added ideas for making bed rest more bearable. I labeled the notebook "The Bed Rest Survival Guide," thinking it might make a good book someday.

After ten weeks of enduring bed rest, my baby's birth no longer could be postponed. Daniel Edward Tracy was born on September 11, 1990, three months too soon. With a critically ill baby in the hospital and some tough times ahead, I filed the bed-rest notebook away.

Two years later, I became pregnant again and was immediately labeled "high risk" because of my pregnancy history. I was instructed to "take it easy and rest frequently." If bleeding began (and it did), I was to go directly to bed.

Bed rest was certainly difficult the first time around, but with an energetic toddler now in tow, it seemed impossible. This time, though, I knew firsthand what a premature birth would mean to my baby and family's future. I would much rather be the incubator on the couch than have my baby in an incubator in the intensive-care nursery, and so I tapped into every support system I could find, surrounding myself with supportive friends and family.

And, I took more notes.

On April 18, 1993, Steven James Tracy was born full term and perfect. Happy and grateful to have my two boys, and knowing firsthand how important it is for a baby to develop and grow within the womb, I soon began offering support to high-risk moms through hospital visits, telephone calls, and by writing articles. Many of the sections in this book evolved out of listening to the concerns and needs of these women over the last decade (in addition to my early note taking, of course).

The birth of this book is truly a labor of love. My hope is that you will let these pages be your guiding light during your bed-rest journey. I hope you'll keep this book by your bedside and refer to it often for direction, comfort, and encouragement.

And when your bundle of joy is in your arms and you're back on your feet, I hope you'll send me a birth announcement.

CHAPTER ONE

When the Rx Is Bed Rest

I never knew anyone who had a complicated pregnancy. All around me, at work, in my family, at the gym, women conceived easily, carried to term, and delivered adorable, healthy infants. My sister-in-law, Kirsten, made it look easy. Within ten years, she became the mother of six beautiful, full-term children, including a set of surprise twins. So, understandably, when my pregnancy test came back positive, I had great expectations, and I eagerly began making plans.

First, I wrote a long to-do list of job-related tasks I needed to complete before my maternity leave. (It never crossed my mind that I might not work all nine months!) Next, I signed up for an exercise class for expectant women to ensure that I'd stay fit throughout my prenatal period. On the weekends, I planned to shop for maternity clothes and baby necessities, as well as remodel the guest room into a nursery.

Imagine my shock when I began spotting heavily during my eighteenth week and my doctor prescribed "limited bed rest"—no going to the office and very little household activity. Like Alice in Wonderland falling down the rabbit's hole, my world began spinning out of control.

How would I tell my boss that I needed time off (in addition to my maternity leave), and that I didn't know when I'd return? If I lost my full-time salary, how would my husband, George, and I cover the bills, including a brand-new mortgage? With George traveling several days a week on business, and no family nearby, how was I *really* supposed to stay in bed? Who would make meals and do laundry? Added to all these questions was an even more alarming one: Would my baby be okay?

If you've recently been given bed-rest orders, these questions and more are probably running through your mind right now. You're feeling stressed, to say the least. Take a deep breath . . . and another . . . and another. . . . Find comfort in knowing that many women before you have been banished to bed (experts estimate up to 700,000 each year; that's one in five expectant women!), and many are rewarded with healthy, full-term babies.

Some of these women, including myself, will share our stories throughout these pages, helping you feel less alone. We'll also share our strategies for surviving—and thriving—during the bed-rest experience. Though a complicated pregnancy was certainly one of the most difficult experiences we've faced in life, each of us discovered it was also an opportunity—a time for personal growth, reflection, and a chance to discover who we really are as women, wives, daughters, and mothers.

So, beginning right now, let us guide, comfort, and inspire you during your bed-rest journey.

WHY LIE LOW?

As you now know, when a pregnancy becomes complicated, bed rest is often prescribed as part of treatment. Gravity is the underlying medical reason: The earth's gravity pulls on different parts of your body when you are lying down than when you are standing up. Many obstetricians believe that using gravity through a lying-down position aids in stabilizing or improving some medical conditions.

Limiting physical activity may also reduce stress on the heart, improve blood flow to the kidneys (eliminating excess fluids), and increase circulation to the uterus (providing additional oxygen and nutrients to your baby). Lying low may take pressure off your cervix (the neck of the womb), and less activity conserves your energy, allowing more nutrition from the foods you eat to go directly toward your baby's growth.

Obstetricians also prescribe bed rest because they want to do everything possible to help you have a healthy baby, and they want you and your family to feel that you're doing everything possible, too. Though you may read reports that question whether bed rest really works, keep in mind that, at present, there is no way of knowing which woman and baby may benefit from bed rest.

All obstetricians do acknowledge that the longer a baby is in the womb, the better chance for a healthy birth. A premature baby, born before thirty-seven weeks of gestation, is at risk for breathing and feeding difficulties and developmental delays. The earlier the baby arrives, the greater the likelihood of problems. With this in mind, most women facing a high-risk pregnancy are more than willing to put their lives on hold if it even *slightly* increases the chance of delivering a healthy baby.

You may have been prescribed bed rest for one or more of the following complications: vaginal bleeding; placenta previa (when the placenta partially or completely covers the cervix); placenta abruption (a separation of the placenta from the uterine wall); high blood pressure (pregnancy-induced hypertension or preeclampsia); an incompetent cervix (the cervix shortens without contractions); premature labor; intrauterine growth retardation (the baby is small for gestational age); multiple babies; or a chronic health problem. Additional treatment may include labor-inhibiting drugs, called tocolytics, or using a beltlike monitor to send contraction reports to your doctor. If your blood pressure is high, you may need to track it with a blood-pressure cuff. Women with gestational diabetes often need to take glucose tests.

Your doctor should thoroughly explain your medical condition and treatment. To complement your doctor's care, a list of books on high-risk pregnancy is included at the end of this chapter; additional resources can be found under Complications in Pregnancy and Health Web Sites in appendix D.

When learning about your pregnancy, do not hesitate to ask as many questions as needed. Your doctor should understand that a complicated pregnancy and bed-rest prescription are extremely stressful. If he doesn't, look for a more empathetic health-care provider, as you'll be working closely together over the next months. If you have any concerns about your care or bed-rest instructions, seek a second opinion, preferably from a perinatologist (an obstetrician who specializes in high-risk pregnancies). The American College of Obstetricians and Gynecologists can refer you to an expert in your area (see Who Can Help at the end of this chapter).

As you gather information about your pregnancy and health care, keep a notebook, or write down notes in the margins and appendices A and B. I tracked important information, such as bed-rest instructions, names and phone numbers, and dates and times of any unusual symptoms, throughout each of my pregnancies. One of the Bed Rest Book Buddies, Rachel, noted contractions in a tiny spiral notebook and wrote down when she took her two medications. "Bed rest numbs the brain, and I could never remember which medication I took last," she says.

Understanding your pregnancy and why you should lie low—how bed rest may help your baby—will give you peace of mind, as Erin, a two-time bed-rest veteran, learned:

I started labor at eighteen weeks during my first pregnancy and was incredibly scared every time I contracted. I wasn't told that preterm labor didn't necessarily mean immediate delivery. I flinched every time I contracted—and that was six to ten times an hour! If I'd been told that by catching my early labor the contractions could probably be controlled, I would have felt less crazy.

During Erin's second pregnancy, when she again experienced premature labor, being informed helped her feel less anxious. "I knew much more about preterm labor," says Erin. "I felt completely comfortable and confident that my doctors were doing everything possible for me and my baby."

UNDERSTANDING YOUR LIMITATIONS

I didn't get clearly defined limits. I was told to slow down and not lift my fourteen-month-old. I felt like I was supposed to do something without full instructions, which normally wouldn't have bothered me except this time my baby's life was on the line. I was terrified of failing and having her early.

⌐ Erin

Just as each pregnancy is unique, each bed-rest prescription, based on that doctor's beliefs and practices, is different. Limitations can range from some activity restriction and periods of lying down (modified or limited bed rest), to complete bed rest at home (lying down with no bathroom privileges), to bed rest in a hospital. Bed-rest prescriptions can change during pregnancy, too.

> *I was told no housework or cooking, to lie down often, and put my feet up when sitting. I could go on three outings a week in a wheelchair.*
>
>   ⌒ Lisa

> *After my cerclage placement at fifteen weeks, my bed-rest prescription was modified. I could get up four to six hours in the morning, then down for the rest of the day. My doctor's orders were to "listen to my body."*
>
>   ⌒ Rachel

> *When I was at home, I was on complete bed rest, which I understood as sitting all the time except for bathroom breaks. I could take the steps once a day. I got out of the house once a week for doctors' visits. I did borrow a wheelchair for these visits because every time I stood I contracted.*
>
>   *In the hospital, I was completely horizontal except for meals. I was not allowed to shower (I took one every three*

weeks!). I was so happy when I graduated from a bedpan to a potty chair next to the bed.

                                       ⌒ Leah

I had three confinements. The first time I was placed on restriction at twenty-six weeks when I began to efface and dilate. The second time, at about sixteen weeks, I was told to "put my feet up." Nine weeks later, I was told not to move except to go to the bathroom. The third time I had to be careful and do only light housework, which was hard to comply with because I now had a three- and five-year-old. At twenty-five weeks, I was put in the hospital and given a bedpan.

                                       ⌒ Adrienne

Many women are advised to lie on their sides during bed rest, alternating left and right, to enhance blood supply to the baby. Try not to lie flat on your back: The weight of your baby may put too much pressure on blood vessels in your abdomen, possibly affecting blood pressure and blood flow.

To reduce pressure on the cervix, which can lead to contractions, a woman may be positioned so that her hips are higher than her head (the Trendelenburg position). Hospital beds can easily be placed in this position. At home, the bottom of the bed or couch can be raised using cinder blocks (your doctor will tell you how high). Your health insurance may also cover a hospital bed rental.

Bed-rest restrictions are reduced or lifted when health risks to your baby or you lessen. For example, when your baby reaches a healthy gestational age, you may be allowed to do more, or if your complication, such as preterm labor or bleeding, stops, bed rest may no longer be needed.

Many women on bed rest complain that they don't receive clear bed-rest instructions. Says Leah, "I saw my doctor every two weeks and a high-risk specialist every week and neither explained clearly what bed rest was or what they expected of me." Those who have been hospitalized after modified bed rest, or who were given strict at-home guidelines, often say this experience was less stressful because their limitations were made clear.

My own early bed-rest experience was frustrating. I was told I could work a few hours at home each day, but I never knew how long I should sit at my desk, or how often I could walk up the stairs. I frequently drove to the grocery store and walked to the mailbox (remember, my husband was often away on business), then wondered if I'd done too much.

In retrospect, I should have demanded straightforward guidelines. With this in mind, I've created a checklist of bed-rest restrictions for you, your doctor, or a nurse to complete (see appendix A, Your Bed Rest Checklist). Make several copies for updating as your pregnancy progresses. Also, consider posting this list by your bedside as a friendly reminder to visitors of your limitations. Remember, too, to listen to your body: If something doesn't feel right, don't do it.

WORKING WITH
YOUR HEALTH-CARE TEAM

A nurse called me every morning and I found it reassuring. Home health-care nurses came three times a week. Their visits were helpful because I was reassured that everything was medically fine, and I also really enjoyed the company!

⌐ Teri

It takes a team to care for a bed-rest pregnancy. Players most commonly include your doctor, interns if you're hospitalized in a teaching hospital, nurses, a social worker, a dietitian, a physical therapist, and you and your partner. The roles of experts will be discussed more throughout this book.

You and your partner's role are to be active team players, communicating information about your health, concerns, and feelings to your caregivers. Always keep in mind that you know your body best, and this is your pregnancy and your baby.

Conversely, it's your right to know information pertaining to your health and your baby's health. Some couples want to know every detail of every medical decision; others prefer to know only a limited amount, choosing instead to primarily focus on growing their baby. Let your caregivers know your desires. At times, you may need to be assertive, but by being firm yet polite you should get positive results.

BED REST DOESN'T MEAN BEDRIDDEN

When I first heard my doctor say the words "bed rest" I pictured myself lying in bed wearing one of those dingy, granny bathrobes. The only bedridden people I'd seen were elderly people in nursing homes and several people with chronic illnesses. Fortunately, I ended up spending most of my days on the couch in my sunny family room, surrounded by my loved ones and my favorite things, and wearing normal maternity clothes.

Take note: Bed rest isn't being prescribed because you are sick. You are not limiting your activities and spending time lying down to recover from an illness. What you are doing is *working* to keep your baby from being born too soon—and this job requires a great deal of energy and stamina. You'll need to take good care of yourself, physically and mentally. You'll also need to learn how to maintain your household, nurture your relationships, and successfully get through each day without overtaxing yourself.

There's no doubt about it: Bed rest is hard work. But the rest of this book will show you how to successfully manage your days in waiting with the least amount of stress.

WHO CAN HELP

American College of Obstetricians and Gynecologists
409 12th St., S.W.
Washington, DC 20090
(800) 673-8444 (for an OB/GYN referral, ask for the resource
 center)
www.acog.org

RECOMMENDED READING

Also see appendix D.

Getting Pregnant and Staying Pregnant: Overcoming Infertility and Managing Your High-Risk Pregnancy by Diana Raab, B.S., R.N. (Hunter House, 1999)

A Guide to Effective Care in Pregnancy and Childbirth, 3rd ed., by Murray Enkin, et al. (Oxford University Press, 2000)

The High-Risk Pregnancy Sourcebook by Denise M. Chism (Lowell House, 1998)

How to Prevent Miscarriage and Other Crises of Pregnancy by Stefan Semchyshyn, M.D., and Carol Colman (Macmillan Publishing Co., 1989)

Intensive Caring: New Hope for High-Risk Pregnancy by Dianne Hales and Timothy R. B. Johnson, M.D. (Crown, 1990) (out of print; check your library or used bookstore)

Planning Your Pregnancy and Birth, 3rd ed. (American College of Obstetricians and Gynecologists, 2000)

When Pregnancy Isn't Perfect: A Layperson's Guide to Complications in Pregnancy by Laurie A. Rich (Larata Press, 1998); www.larata.com

CHAPTER TWO

First Things First

I had only been at my job as an editor for two months when I nervously told my boss and coworkers that I was expecting. Just a few days later, I began spotting heavily, and I had to ask a colleague to drive me to the hospital.

Unfortunately, my husband was out of town and couldn't get home until the next day. Without anyone to care for me (my family is spread out from Vermont to Washington state), the doctor insisted I spend the night in the hospital. He also casually mentioned I'd probably have to take some time off of work and lie in bed until the bleeding stopped. If it didn't, I might be spending the rest of my pregnancy on bed rest.

That night I stayed awake thinking of all the arrangements I'd need to make the next day. My husband would have to rearrange his work schedule. I'd have to notify my boss and find out what the company's employee benefits and health insurance covered. We'd have to arrange for friends to help with meals during the day and errands when George traveled.

Once home, I began making phone calls but kept bursting into tears whenever I explained my situation, partly because I didn't know what my situation was! Would I just be taking a few days off from work, or would I be banished to bed until my due date? I felt as though I had no control over my life. I also felt tremendous guilt for causing such upheaval in the lives of so many others.

Although your bed-rest introduction may be different from mine (you may have received strict at-home or hospital bed-rest orders), you are probably feeling very similar emotions and concerns. Parents who have young children at home have added worries.

When trying to accept your complicated pregnancy while making the necessary arrangements, remember the "rest" in bed rest. Try to remain calm and let your partner, friends, colleagues, and family members handle most immediate needs, leaving the less important tasks for later.

If you're single, establishing a network of helpers is critical. Though it may be hard to ask for and accept help, it will be even harder to make the transition from vertical to horizontal living on your own. Swallow your pride and seek assistance. Most people will love to help; they just need to be asked.

To assist you and your helpers, this chapter will walk you through what needs to be done following a bed-rest order.

TELLING YOUR BOSS

My doctor said I'd have to stay home and lie down any time I started spotting. This meant I had to tell my boss and coworkers that I was pregnant much earlier than I'd planned. My boss and colleagues couldn't rely on me to get tasks done because I kept calling in sick, or leaving in the middle of the day, and I never knew how long I'd be out. I'd always been reliable and felt awful about taking so much sick time. Some coworkers became resentful. The women who weren't mothers and even some who were harbored bad feelings for a long time.

⌒ Cathy

After I was released from my first bed-rest episode, I returned to work armed with a blood-pressure cuff. My job typically required a lot of standing, but I was supposed to sit most of the time. I felt like people were judging me; every time I sat down, I felt guilty. Not looking sick didn't help either.

When I was put on bed rest a second time and knew I wouldn't be returning to work, I spent hours at the computer writing instructions for my replacement. I still had to explain everything two or three times on the phone, which was frustrating considering all the time and effort I'd put into making things as easy for her as possible.

⌒ Barb

When you're first given bed-rest orders, you'll need to let your supervisor know immediately that you won't be at work the next day. If you're too upset to call, or want to avoid talking about work concerns, have your partner, a friend, or a family member call. Think twice about talking to coworkers first: You don't want your boss to hear your plans through the office grapevine, creating an atmosphere of distrust. On the other hand, if a coworker is a bed-rest veteran, or has been on disability leave, you may want to discreetly solicit some advice.

If possible, take a few days or so to consider how you'll handle bed rest and your job. You'll need to research your legal rights, your company's employee benefits, and your health-insurance coverage. Consult your employee handbook and talk with the person in your company who handles benefits. Resources at the end of this chapter can also help.

Depending on what limitations your doctor has prescribed (provide your employer with a written note), you may need to go on temporary disability leave, discussed in the next section. Your employer may let you take accumulated sick and vacation days, or unpaid leave, or you may continue working with reduced hours and/or activity restrictions. If you and your boss agree to reduced hours, ask how salary and benefits may be affected.

Once you know how you'd like to handle work, arrange a phone call with your boss and clearly state your medical limitations and work desires. For instance, since my doctor said I could continue editing at home (a job I could easily do in bed), I told my boss I wanted to continue working full time by putting in shorter days and a longer week. Because I didn't know how long I'd be on bed rest, I promised to keep her updated with any medical changes. She seemed to appreciate my honesty. The more helpful and prepared you are, the less resentment coworkers and your boss should harbor.

Once you come to an agreement with your boss, write a memo specifying arrangements, such as the terms of your leave (paid or unpaid), or guidelines for part-time work including how you'll handle communication. You both should sign a letter of agreement and keep a copy.

If you continue working, clearly describe the activity your job requires (standing, sitting, lifting) to your doctor, and ask for guidelines. For example, how long can you sit at a desk, or sit up to use a laptop in bed? Should you eliminate certain household activities to compensate for working? Can you go into the office for an hour once a day or once a week?

If your company has at least fifty employees, you are entitled to twelve weeks of unpaid leave for an illness under the Family and Medical Leave Act (FMLA). Your company may also offer a percentage of earned wages during an FMLA leave. You must have worked for your employer for at least one year and for a minimum of 1,250 hours to qualify. Under this law, your employer must guarantee you'll have the same job, or a similar one with comparable pay and responsibilities, when you return.

Your state may have additional laws regarding parental leave. Changes to the FMLA are being considered at the time of this writing. For more information, consult your company's human resources department or your state's department of labor (see Who Can Help at the end of this chapter).

FILING FOR DISABILITY

If you've been sentenced to complete bed rest, you are now temporarily disabled. Under the Pregnancy Discrimination Act, an employer of fifteen or more workers must treat pregnancy bed rest like any other temporary medical disability. This means you are entitled to the disability leave benefits your company offers. Most state governments also cover temporary disability, and some have leave laws specific to pregnancy-related conditions; consult your state's department of labor (see Who Can Help at the end of this chapter). Be aware that even if you receive disability or unemployment payments, these checks are typically less than your previous wages, and payment doesn't always start right away.

Your supervisor or company's human resources representative can fill you in on the company's disability policy and provide the necessary forms. Don't forget to ask if using disability benefits will affect medical coverage, and if you can use unclaimed sick and vacation days before starting disability.

Notifying Your Health Insurance

A bed-rest pregnancy typically requires more doctor visits, medical tests, and sometimes home-care medical equipment and hospitalization. It's a good idea to understand what your insurance covers so there aren't any billing surprises. A claims counselor who represents your medical insurance will most likely be assigned to your case and can answer questions. If you're not covered by private medical insurance, ask your nurse or doctor to set up a meeting with the social worker at the hospital where you'll deliver.

Should your insurance deny coverage of services or equipment, or deny disability payments, you'll need to stand up for your rights. Bearing in mind that you don't need additional stress, ask for help from your health-care team. You may need to make many phone calls; always ask for the person in charge of making decisions, typically the supervisor. Again, write down any pertinent information, including names, phone numbers, dates, and content of conversations.

Your Partner's Job

Your bed rest will most likely affect your partner's ability to do his job, too, so it's important for him to clearly explain your family's situation to his employer. Consider, too, whether your partner can take some personal time off from work or use sick and vacation days, particularly if you have young children at home to care for. Some fathers arrange to work part time at home for a few days a week or take different shifts, so mom is covered when friends and relatives aren't available for bed-rest duty. Another option may be for dad to take time off under the Family and Medical Leave Act, discussed earlier.

COPING WITH FINANCIAL CONCERNS

For some couples, money problems during bed rest are a source of personal and marital stress. Talking about your concerns can reduce some tension. Discuss which bills to postpone, if a bank or family loan is needed, if dad can work some extra hours or take on a second job, and what items you can do without for a few months.

Some couples who survived bed rest say they were surprised by how much they could actually cut back by packing lunches, making gifts, reducing credit-card purchases, and using coupons. Many also bought baby items at children's consignment stores, rather than department stores, and shopped the Web for bargains.

If necessary, consider renegotiating loans or credit agreements. Creditors have the ability to defer payments, or accept interest-only or partial payments, in special circumstances. The sooner you call a creditor and explain your situation, the better. You should be willing to provide documentation, such as a doctor's prescription or disability papers. Making every effort to work with your creditors should keep your credit rating in good standing.

Your utility companies (telephone, electric, water, gas, sanitation, and even your Internet service provider) may also be willing to renegotiate payments during your bed rest. Again, calling early to discuss options is better than waiting until after a missed payment. When you call, ask to talk to the person who can make such decisions.

Another money-saving option may be a government-funded program called Women, Infants, and Children (WIC) that provides nutritious food to expectant women, based on monthly income level (see Who Can Help at the end of this chapter). You may also qualify for financial assistance from your local township trustee, Medicaid, or Social Security insurance. A federal waiver, called the Katie Beckett Waiver, may be available if you don't qualify for Medicaid or Social Security insurance. Consult your state's department of health and human services (see Who Can Help at the end of this chapter), or contact the social worker or finance office at the hospital where you'll deliver.

If financial concerns have you down, try to remember your pregnancy lasts just nine months, not a lifetime. You can catch up on those bills once your baby arrives.

FINDING CHILD CARE

I was put on complete bed rest at twenty-one weeks. This was so difficult with a two-year-old at home! I had planned on quitting my job in a month, so we had no day care arranged. What a scramble to find someone to come help me! I knew I had to have full-time help because my belly turned hard as a rock every time I stood.

                                    ⌒ Leah

My mother lives a mile away and on a beach. She picked up my four-year-old and drove him to her house every day. My sisters and sisters-in-law took turns watching him. I had the peace of mind that he was having a great time with his cousins and a normal summer.

                                    ⌒ Kendra

If you have young children at home, you'll most likely have to make part-time or full-time child-care arrangements. Transportation for school-age children may also be needed. Understandably, it's hard to make arrangements when you don't know how long you'll need help. As one mother says, "The job would last anywhere from a few weeks to permanent. How would we find someone under those stipulations?" Short-term solutions to your care-giving and transportation problems may be necessary until long-term arrangements can be worked out.

Working mothers sometimes have an advantage over stay-at-home moms because they can often continue prearranged child care while on bed rest (though financial restrictions may prevent some from doing so). Additional baby-sitting may be needed at night and on the weekends. To determine what child-care arrangements will work best for your family, consider these questions:

- Can we continue to pay for our current day-care/school arrangements?

- Do any special arrangements, such as transportation, need to be made regarding our present day-care/school arrangements?

- Can we afford to pay for full-time day care?

- Will part-time help at home be enough? If so, about how many hours do we need?

- Would we prefer child care in our home, at a home-based day care, or at a child-care center?

- Can I get adequate rest with my child at home, or would it be better if my child leaves for part of the day?

- Can relatives or friends living nearby help?

- Can a relative or friend temporarily live with us?

- Is there a stay-at-home mom in the neighborhood who may be willing to help?

• Can we use a mother's helper or young baby-sitter, or do we need someone who is more mature?

• Are there any camps or programs for my child during holiday or summer breaks? (Check with local child-care centers, YMCAs, and recreation services.)

At the end of this chapter is a list of several resources to help you locate local day-care centers and child-care services. You can also consult your local newspaper's classifieds, child-care listings in your telephone book, or schools for names of students who have passed a qualified baby-sitting course. Help may also be found at a local college's student employment office, or a high school's student volunteer office. Also, consider placing ads in churches' and civic organizations' newsletters.

Many mothers who thought bed rest would be impossible with young children at home found creative, budget-minded child-care solutions. One mom traded baby-sitting; she promised to watch another mom's kids after the baby was born. Another mom utilized a Girl Scout troop. Religious and service groups, such as United Way, may have programs to help those in need. Your local department of social services (check your telephone book), or the social worker at the hospital where you'll likely deliver, should have contact information and more ideas.

For older children who need to get to after-school and weekend activities, a car pool may be necessary. When you explain your dilemma, most people will be anxious to help, and you can taxi their kids once you're back on your feet. Also, consider paying a mature teen or college student to shuttle your youngsters.

CREATING A COMMUNITY PREGNANCY

My bed rest was truly a community effort. My mom and dad took over caring for my children, my best friend arranged movie nights at my house, and another friend, who'd been on bed rest before, brought me books.

People I know in town and through my kids' schools called, visited, helped with child care, and offered to set up a regular meal-delivery schedule. I really felt like everyone I knew had a hand in helping with my pregnancy.

⌒ Kendra

For many women, it's very difficult to ask for and accept a helping hand. How we're raised, our culture, and our own beliefs often make it difficult for us to reach out. I remember after my first son was born, several neighbors told me they didn't even know I was pregnant (because I didn't tell them!). They were further shocked when I told them I'd spent most of the pregnancy in bed.

When complications arose during my next pregnancy, I had a large network of support from various mothers' groups to rely on. Needless to say, my second complicated pregnancy was much more bearable than the first.

Deborah S. Simmons, a licensed marriage and family therapist and a bed-rest veteran, says that a woman on bed rest should create a "community pregnancy" by allowing others to have a stake in her child's birth. "You have to be willing to talk about your bed-rest pregnancy outside of the house and actively seek help," she says. "This means letting your church, clubs, volunteer groups, coworkers—anyone you have associations with—know you need assistance. If someone offers a hand, you must take it."

You'll probably find that most people are delighted to help when asked. They'll also appreciate specific suggestions of what to do, as Erin discovered: "I tried to be explicit about how people could help out. Take me to the doctor's. Take the kids for a walk. Pick up certain items at the grocery store. Or just come by and sit with me. Many people want to help, but don't know how."

If you feel sheepish about asking for help, remember that you can pay back the kindnesses of others after your baby arrives. Like the women in this book, you may even find yourself helping other women on bed rest. After all, those of us who have survived bed rest know the value of a community pregnancy!

Who Can Help

Also see Bed Rest/Support in appendix D.

For child-care information:

National Association of Child Care Resource and Referral Agencies

1319 F St., N.W., Suite 500

Washington, DC 20004

(202) 393-5501

(800) 570-4543

www.naccrra.net

Other child-care Web sites:

www.carefinder.com

www.edaycare.com

For employment information:

Families and Work Institute

330 Seventh Ave., 14th Floor

New York, NY 10001

(212) 465-2044

www.familiesandwork.org

9to5, National Association of Working Women

231 W. Wisconsin Ave., Suite 900

Milwaukee, WI 53203

(414) 274-0925

(800) 522-0925 (job problem hot line)

http://feminist.com/9to5.htm

NOW Legal Defense and Education Fund

395 Hudson St.

New York, NY 10014

(212) 925-6635

www.nowldef.org

lir@nowldef.org (legal information and referral service)

United States Department of Labor

Office of Public Affairs

200 Constitution Ave., N.W., Room S-1032

Washington, DC 20210

(202) 693-4650

www.dol.gov

www.dol.gov/dol/esa/public/contacts/state_of.htm (state labor offices)

For financial information and assistance:

National Foundation for Credit Counseling

801 Roeder Road, Suite 900

Silver Spring, MD 20910

(301) 589-5600

(800) 388-2227 (crisis hot line)

www.nfcc.org

Women, Infants, and Children (WIC)
USDA Food and Nutrition Service
3101 Park Center Drive, Room 819
Alexandria, VA 22302
(703) 305-2286
www.fns.usda.gov/wic
(They will provide WIC information for your state and a toll-free
    telephone number.)

For health-care information:
National health-care policy updates:
www.familiesusa.org

National Maternal & Child Health Clearinghouse
2070 Chain Bridge Road, Suite 450
Vienna, VA 22182
(888) 434-4MCH ((888) 434-4624)
www.nmchc.org
(They will provide two-page summaries of mother and baby
    health-related contacts by state.)

United States Department of Health and Human Services
200 Independence Ave., S.W.
Washington, DC 20201
(877) 696-6775
www.hhs.gov
www.hhs.gov/about/regionmap.html (regional offices)

CHAPTER THREE

Setting Up Shop

Once you've started to accept your bed-rest situation and have made the initial arrangements, you'll need to think more about your resting location: where you'll bide your time for the next days, weeks, or months. Before you jump into bed or on the couch, consider these three important factors: 1. your restrictions (Can you spend part of the day up and about, or are you completely tied down?); 2. your home's layout (Can you get to the bathroom and answer the door without climbing stairs?); and 3. your children and pets (What part of the house allows you to adequately care for them?).

The first time I was sentenced to a short bed rest, I served time in our master bedroom with an attached bathroom. However, it was rather dark and depressing, and I hated being so far away from the day-to-day activity that took place downstairs. So, when I was ordered to bed a second time and for a longer duration, I camped out on the couch in our family room. This room had three large picture windows framing views of the Rocky Mountains, providing me with many hours of pleasure.

When planning your bed-rest location, it may help to think of it as your command post: It should give you the most influence over your daily living. Consider the area's proximity to the bathroom and kitchen, its lighting and temperature, and the availability of a telephone and entertainment items (television, VCR/DVD, computer, stereo, and radio). Also, think about what other activities the room is used for and how comfortable you will feel resting there (for example, the kids' playroom may be too noisy and stressful).

Many women set up two bed-rest locations: the bedroom and another room in the house. Erin spent her mornings on the couch downstairs and afternoons in her bed upstairs. "My husband carried my toddler down in the mornings so we could be together and have access to his toys and the kitchen," she says. "Then my mother's helper carried him back upstairs for naps."

Sara spent most of her three-month bed rest in her bedroom. "I taped cards from people on the walls to cheer me up, and I brought the outdoors inside with lots of plants," she says. Two foldaway card tables by her bedside and several large plastic see-through bins kept necessities within arm's reach.

With permission from her doctor, Jackie rested at her mother's nearby beach house every few days. "It was nice because I got to look at someone else's ceiling for a while," she says. "My mom has air-conditioning, too, and in July and August on the East Coast that was a real luxury."

If your doctor agrees and the weather permits, spend some time reclining outdoors. Says Allison, "The sun's warmth on my face, the sound of birds, watching the clouds, even if just for twenty minutes, put me in a better mood."

BUILDING YOUR BED-REST NEST

When a mother bird builds a nest, she searches for the most perfect of nature's materials to create it. Your "nest" requires the same loving attention. The more content and comfortable you are, the easier complying with bed rest will be. Here are some ideas from bed-rest veterans for nesting materials:

- Lots of pillows. Select those with different shapes and firmness for your head, neck, back, legs, and belly. Many women recommend full-body pillows, too.

- Your best and favorite bedding. My mom sent me a pillowcase with funny cartoon dogs that made me smile throughout the day. Scented fabric spray can give your linens a fresh smell.

- A container for water and a drinking cup are mandatory. To prevent spills, many women on bed rest use large insulated cups with lids and straws. Keep in mind that you should drink at least eight glasses of water per day.

· A small refrigerator or a cooler for drinks, snacks, and meals.

· A tray or table to support meals. Some bed trays can be found for less than $15 at discount stores.

· A lap desk or clipboard for writing.

· A cordless telephone if you're not near a phone jack, as well as your personal telephone directory and a local telephone book. An answering machine or service is also helpful when you're not up to or available for talking.

· A baby monitor, walkie-talkies, or intercom for communicating to family members and household help (they're great for checking on older kids, too). A bell to signal that you need assistance can also be useful.

· Toiletry items in a makeup case, such as a comb and brush, lotion, fingernail file, tissues, lip balm, and anything else that may tempt you to get up.

· Many women who rest in bed recommend egg-crate mattresses. If your doctor prescribes a therapeutic mattress, check to see if your insurance will cover its cost. Several of the women in this book loved their waterbeds during bed rest.

- Entertainment items, including a television program guide, remote controls for TV and VCR/DVD, a Walkman and tapes, writing supplies, reading materials, and handwork.

- A computer and Internet access. If you don't have a computer, is it possible to borrow one from your partner's office, a family member, or a friend? Some nonprofit organizations have lending programs, and some companies lease at reasonable rates. Though a computer is an expensive extra, it can offer you hours of entertainment and much-needed support. A few hospitals are even starting to see the benefits and providing patients with laptops.

- Some sort of table to place items in reach. An ironing board that can be adjusted for height works well.

- A container for supplies (crafts, reading material, scissors, pens and paper, etc.). A hanging shoe rack with pockets and a three-tiered storage shelf on wheels are two good choices.

LYING LOW WITH KIDS

No doubt about it: Bed rest is toughest on families with young children. My "house arrest" was certainly more difficult to adhere to when I had a two-year-old to care for than when I was expecting my first. But what made it doable was setting up a toddler-friendly bed-rest nest.

When setting up shop, consider your child's safety. Remove objects that your child could knock over or climb on, tape electrical cords down to the floor, plug outlets, and utilize baby gates. Eliminate items your child could choke on or break.

With young children who need more care, moms need to get down to their level, thus avoiding having to pick them up or bend down. Some moms place regular or inflatable mattresses on the floor. A low cot or a foam chair that rolls out can work, too.

Caregiving and entertainment also need consideration. Meals, snacks, bottles, and drinks can be stored with mom's food in a cooler or bedside basket. A child who normally eats in a highchair needs a closer-to-the-ground feeding chair. A toddler may do fine using mom's bedside table or a child-size table and chair. To reach fallen, out-of-reach items, a mechanical grabber, available in many toy stores, can be useful (but get used to Cheerios and cookie crumbs on the floor!).

Diapers, children's books, and toys can be kept in bedside storage bins and baskets. A small wagon that your children can pull will help them bring items to you. Hanging shoe pockets hung on the wall or door is great for older kids' art supplies.

If you have school-age children, having a homework table or desk in your room can help you participate. A calendar of activities and school events, as well as a place for school papers, will not only help you stay on top of things, but make your children feel that you're still involved in their lives.

*To keep little fingers away from my medication, we pur-
chased a cash box with a lock and kept all medical supplies
and drugs in it. I kept my daily supply of medications on a
small ice pack in the box. We taped the key on the bathroom
mirror out of reach from curious toddlers, but still accessible
to the home-care nurses.*

⌒ Erin

CREATING A ROUTINE

Many at-home and hospitalized women on bed rest find that
sticking to a schedule for meals, personal grooming, naps, and visits
makes the time go by faster. If you're allowed to get up for part of the
day, you'll want to utilize that time efficiently; a schedule can help.

Writing down your routine will help family members and friends
plan around meals, naps, medical tests, and even favorite TV programs. If you like, post your schedule near your bedside. The following is one mother's schedule during at-home bed rest:

8:00 A.M.   Breakfast in bed with Richard and children.

8:30 A.M.   Baby-sitter from local college arrives.

9:00 A.M.   Take blood pressure.

9:15 A.M.   If blood pressure is okay, take a shower and get dressed.

10:00 A.M.   Read newspaper and magazines; order books from library; call some friends.

10:30 A.M.   Listen to relaxation tape.

11:30 A.M.   Move to couch downstairs; have lunch with kids.

12:00 P.M.   Watch TV news and do light exercises (see chapter 6).

1:00 P.M.   Take nap.

2:00 P.M.   Make telephone calls (doctor's appointment, health insurance, mothers of multiples club). Write grocery list; cut coupons; look for some easy recipes for Richard.

3:00 P.M.   Monitor blood pressure; watch *Oprah*.

4:00 P.M.   Baby-sitter leaves. Time for children's hour! Do new puzzle, color, and play cards.

5:00 P.M.   Watch video with kids.

6:00 P.M.   Richard home; casserole from church group.

7:00 P.M.   Back to bed. Play charades; read to kids.

8:00 P.M.   Watch television and address baby announcements.

9:00 P.M.   Monitor blood pressure. Talk to my baby.

10:00 P.M.   Sleep.

Planning activities for a week or month ahead can also help you manage your time. On your monthly calendar, write in your medical appointments, including expected sonograms and any medical procedures, when relatives are arriving to help, date nights with your husband, and movie-and-pizza nights with girlfriends.

RUNNING YOUR HOUSEHOLD

I used the same volunteers to run the same errands each week so they could do them at their convenience. That way I also didn't feel like I was bugging them.

— Allison

We made duplicates of our house key for regular visitors and household help. We also hid a copy in a safe place near our door so I wouldn't have to get up when friends wanted to drop by.

— Erin

I'm an obsessively organized, neat person. An example: One of the first projects I wanted to do during bed rest was clean out my bathroom drawers. But I quickly learned to lessen my housekeeping standards while horizontal and let George and my helpers handle things their way. I still have the pink cotton sweater George washed and dried—and miniaturized!—as a reminder of his well-intentioned efforts.

If you have household help, paid or volunteer, chances are they won't do the job the way you would. Nor will your partner, mother, or mother-in-law. Having people in your home, doing the tasks you normally do, may also feel intrusive and make you uncomfortable. Try to relax. It bears repeating: Bed rest is short-term. You can find those misplaced dishes and get rid of that dust once you're back on your feet.

What may help you to feel more in control is jotting down specific things you'd like others to do. Also, if small projects you can do from bed won't cause added stress, do them. Many women on bed rest organize files, fold socks, mend clothes—and clean out bathroom drawers. One mom I know even ironed in bed using a portable ironing board.

> *I rolled all our coins from our banks, did our taxes, balanced my husband's checkbook (it was full of errors!), and helped my kids with their homework.*
>
> ⌒ Kendra

Remember, though, that everything will take a little longer when you're lying horizontal. Don't set unreasonable deadlines or goals that may only cause frustration and added stress.

BOREDOM BUSTERS

At first I thought it would be nice to be pampered and to watch television all day. But I didn't feel pampered, and television got old really fast.

◜ Barb

There are certain things that I could never have done until my children were much older because I never would have taken the time. However, on bed rest, I taught myself how to play bridge and to knit. I never did finish the baby blanket I started, but it sure made me feel like I was doing something special for my baby.

◜ Leah

My sole journeys were on Mondays when I went to my obsterician's office. Driving my car seemed acutely interesting, the sky seemed bluer than blue, and I loved watching how the world was changing around me, going from fall to winter. It seemed peculiar to talk with people in the doctor's office, almost like watching myself in a movie.

◜ Leslie

Anyone who has been on bed rest knows it's anything but restful. You have way too much time to worry about your baby, family, job, finances, housekeeping, even how you're going to get your next meal. When you're not worrying, you're watching the clock or too many TV talk shows.

To combat my worrying and boredom, I made a long list of things I wanted to do during my "time off." To name a few: write a novel, read the classics, learn to knit, study Spanish, and write a letter to everyone in my address book. Did I do any of these? No.

Typically, I'm the type of person who always has to be doing something, even when sitting. So, it really surprised me that I spent so much time just staring at the television (those talk shows just made me feel more depressed). I felt lazy and guilty for not doing more, but it seemed like it took all of my energy just to get through each hour and each day, and I had very little left for other activities.

"You shouldn't feel obligated to be productive," says Mara Stein, a clinical psychologist who spent six weeks on hospital bed rest. "Certainly do things that appeal to you, but remember you're doing an enormous job just by staying in bed."

Some days you may feel like accomplishing more; other days you may just want to lie there. Do what's right for you. When you'd like an idea for passing the time, here are some suggestions from bed-rest veterans:

- Update your address book and address thank-you notes, birth announcements, and holiday cards (no matter what the month is).

- Start your baby's photo album with ultrasound pictures and pregnancy shots.

- Research your family tree by writing letters to relatives, looking up information on the Internet, and using library resources.

- Write letters to your unborn baby.

- Get a card-game book from the library and learn some new games. Teach them to your children or to friends who visit. Learn all the versions of solitaire.

- Make some needlepoint holiday gifts.

- Learn to knit and make a blanket for your baby.

- Borrow your child's hand-held computer game.

- Watch childbirth education videos, or arrange for a childbirth educator to come to your home. Your library, video store, or hospital may rent or lend labor-and-delivery and parenting tapes.

- Learn a second language. Most libraries have tapes and books to teach you.

- Pamper yourself with a manicure.

- If you've already read all the books in the house, try something different. Read all the books from one author. Try a new genre, or read a mystery series.

- Do a jigsaw puzzle and glue it together with special puzzle glue.

- Organize your recipe collection, or start a new one.

- With a friend's help, experiment with a new look for your hair and makeup.

- Volunteer. Many nonprofit groups need help making telephone calls or addressing envelopes.

- Try sketching or cartooning.

- Get a book about birds and, using binoculars, try to identify some outside your window.

- Shop by phone for personal services, such as the bank with the highest interest rates, better loan rates, or prices of new tires for your car.

- Clip coupons and start a coupon-filing system.

- Create a family budget and filing system (include receipts from bed-rest expenses, such as child care and household help; they may be tax deductible). Do some financial planning.

- Send away for catalogs. Even if you don't order anything, they're fun to browse through.

- Learn and practice calligraphy.

- Surprise your partner by learning about his favorite sport or hobby.

- See if the local library has a service for the home-bound; they may deliver books through the mail or volunteers.

ONE DAY AT A TIME

Bed rest will be the hardest thing you'll ever do. It is tough emotionally. It requires humility because of all the help you need, and stamina like you've never had to demonstrate before. However, achieving a successful bed rest is a sacrifice you're making for your child. No matter what, remember that the number of days you are on bed rest is limited to the length of your pregnancy. It does not last forever!

⌒ Kendra

When many women and their partners who survived bed rest are asked, How did you do it? they often reply, By taking it one day at a time. Thinking of bed rest in terms of a trimester, a month, or even a few weeks can seem overwhelming, even impossible. Getting through the day is much more manageable, and you may be surprised by how quickly those days will add up.

It's important to celebrate each day that you and your family manage bed rest. Check off the passing day on a calendar using a V for victory. You should celebrate each passing week, too, with a special treat (a yummy dessert, a pedicure from a friend, or a massage from a loved one). Focusing on the present doesn't mean you shouldn't daydream about the future, however. Says Kendra, "Keep thinking about all the things you'll do when your bed rest is over, because, believe it or not, that day will come."

WHO CAN HELP

Keep track of important names and telephone numbers in appendix B, Names, Numbers, and Notes. Also see Who Can Help at the end of chapter 5 for meal-related services. If you're not online, your telephone directory can be a valuable resource.

Bill paying:
bills.yahoo.com
www.checkfree.com
www.paymybills.com

Book reviews:
www.bookbrowser.com
www.bookwire.com
www.nyt.com/books

Bookstores on-line:

www.amazon.com

www.barnesandnoble.com

www.booksamillion.com

www.powells.com

Craft ideas and supplies:

www.artstore.com

www.craftopia.com

www.craftsetc.com

www.craftsinc.com

www.michaels.com

Learn to knit and crochet:

www.craftyarncouncil.com

Maternity wear:

www.annacris.com

www.apeainthepod.com

www.lizlange.com

www.thatglow.com

Maternity wear (secondhand):

www.littledeals.com

www.motshop.com

Prescription drug delivery:

www.drugstore.com

www.rx.com

Recorded books:

(800) 638-1304

www.recordedbooks.com

Rental videos:

www.bigstar.com

www.netflix.com

Stamps by phone:

(800) STAMP24 ((800) 782-6724)

CHAPTER FOUR

When Hospitalization Is Needed

Your bed rest may have started in the hospital, or pregnancy complications may make a trip necessary. I was hospitalized for a few days, once for unexplained bleeding and another time for high blood pressure. Barb was admitted several times to monitor and control her high blood pressure. Danielle went into labor at twenty-six weeks and was hospitalized for the remainder of her twin pregnancy.

Whether for a night, several days, or for weeks, hospitalization can create tremendous stress for you and your family. However, on a positive note, some women say that getting full-service and around-the-clock hospital care can be comforting. "At home, I was always worrying about whether I'd recognize the signs of labor or another serious symptom," says Allison. "In the hospital, with doctors and nurses watching twenty-four hours a day and with all the monitors, I felt more relaxed and reassured that my baby would be okay."

This chapter will help you prepare for a possible hospital stay and cope if you are admitted. If you've just begun reading this book from a hospital bed and turned to this chapter, you're in the right place. However, once you've finished, go back to chapter 1; most topics addressed throughout this book apply to both hospital and at-home bed rest.

What to Pack (Just in Case)

I only had my purse and clothes on my back when my doctor ordered me to go to the hospital. I am one of those people who carries her life in a suitcase, so it was hard for me to be away from home without making preparations.

— Nina

You may want to pack a hospital bag just in case the unexpected happens. Some mothers take an overnight bag to every doctor's appointment. If you like to be prepared, or you're currently in the hospital trying to think of what you need from home, here is a helpful checklist:

_____   maternity bras and panties

_____   nightgown and bathrobe

_____   slippers, comfortable slip-on shoes, and socks

_____   toiletries (brush, comb, toothbrush, toothpaste, hand-held mirror, makeup, shampoo and rinse, lotion, perfume, travel hair dryer, lip balm)

_____ telephone directory (the hospital may or may not provide one) and address book

_____ several clothes hangers

_____ your own pillow with an identifiable pillowcase and a favorite blanket or comforter

_____ a change purse and lots of quarters for snacks and sundries (do not keep large bills in your room)

_____ the book you were reading or a craft project you were working on

_____ a calendar and a clock

_____ family pictures

_____ ear plugs and eye shades (many women swear by these!)

_____ this book, your favorite pregnancy book, and your pregnancy notebook

AN UNEXPECTED TRIP

"Shocked and confused" is how Leah described her feelings when her doctor said "I'm admitting you." "I couldn't believe this was really happening to me and my baby," says Leah.

Learning you need hospital care is frightening, to say the least. Along with extreme concern about your baby's health, you may also be worried about how your hospitalization will affect your other children, your partner, your job, your house, and your other obligations.

Checking in to the hospital can be disorienting. You may not even remember how you got there or the admission process. You may feel lightheaded, confused, and find it difficult to answer questions.

Right now, the best thing you can do for your baby and yourself is to get through this day and let others help you do it. The nurse in your doctor's office, your partner, a family member, or a friend can make phone calls and arrangements (refer to chapter 2). Accept all offers of help, and try not to think too far ahead. If needed, you can work out long-term arrangements later.

Once you're in bed and the health-care staff has evaluated and treated you, your room will become less chaotic. Now you can start focusing on getting settled. The following are suggestions from bed-rest veterans for adjusting to your home away from home:

· Take deep breaths and try to remain calm. Remind yourself that you are in the best place, getting the best care, for your baby.

- Ask a nurse for paper and make a list of items you want from home (see What to Pack (Just in Case) on page 50). For the time being, the hospital will provide you with essentials, such as a toothbrush, toothpaste, and a comb.

- If you don't have a room with a window, request one. Open the shades so you know the time of day, helping you feel less out of touch.

- You may like the television or radio on (some women find watching a familiar show or the news comforting). Or, you may prefer silence. Health-care providers may require that your room stays quiet and calm, especially if you're on medications or your blood pressure is high.

- If you're admitted to a room on the maternity floor, and you have a new mother for a roommate, or if the sounds of babies or women delivering are upsetting you, ask to change rooms. If you encounter obstacles, ask your doctor or the hospital social worker for assistance.

- Admission to the hospital is exhausting. If you'd like to take a nap, tell a nurse.

- If you've missed a meal during the admission process, request a snack. Your partner or the person who brought you to the hospital may like one, too.

- You may need to request a telephone in your room. However, this is not the time to start calling everyone.

- Inquire about visiting hours. If you have other children, ask specifically about children's visiting hours.

- Don't be surprised if you don't remember a lot of your doctor's instructions or explanations. This is a stressful time. Having to ask for explanations repeatedly is understandable. Write down any important information.

- Remember, the nurses are there for you: Don't hesitate to ask for items you need, or to talk to them about any concerns.

THE FIRST FEW DAYS

The first three days of being in the hospital were just awful. After that, I realized I shouldn't waste my time focusing on the bad. If I wasted days not sleeping or eating, I could hurt my baby's chances.

— Leah

Adjusting to hospital life will take *at least* a few days. Then you'll start getting used to the daily routine: when the nurses take your vital signs, when your doctor visits, the approximate time meals and snacks are delivered, and when medications are given. Family and friends may start visiting or calling more regularly. You'll have some of your personal items, and you'll feel slightly more at ease.

You'll still be very concerned about your baby's well-being, but a routine, knowing what to expect each day, can lessen some anxiety. Consultations with hospital staff (a high-risk obstetrician, a dietitian, a physical therapist, an occupational therapist, a social worker, or a clergy person) can also relieve some concerns and fears.

After a few days, if not sooner, you'll know more about your condition and treatment. You may have had medical tests or even surgery, been prescribed medications, or directed to lie in a certain position. Depending on your health and your baby's health, plans for treatment may now include going home to bed rest, remaining in the hospital for a short time, or staying until delivery. (If you're expecting an extended stay, go to the next section, Surviving an Extended Stay.)

If you're being discharged, congratulations! Remember, however, that making homecoming plans can be burdensome. Ask a family member or a friend to take care of arrangements (refer to chapters 2 and 3). Most importantly, try to stay calm and relaxed.

Before you're released, a nurse or your doctor will discuss any pertinent information with you, such as medication to take, symptoms to look for, and special instructions for follow-up care. If a new bed-rest order is being prescribed, use the checklist in appendix A to get clear instructions.

If your insurance covered a special mattress or other supplies during your hospitalization, be sure to take them home with you. Also, write the names and phone numbers of any specialists you saw in the hospital in appendix B. Don't hesitate to call them should any questions arise following homecoming.

On the way home, the fresh air and outdoor sights will feel wonderful. You may be tempted to visit a friend, stop at the store, or get that fast-food meal you've been craving. Remember, you're not leaving the hospital because you've recovered, but because your doctor believes your pregnancy can be managed at home. Save your energy for adjusting to bed rest at home.

SURVIVING AN EXTENDED STAY

I planned to go to the hospital for a day, maybe overnight, so I was shocked when my doctor said, "You're in here until you deliver."

⟜ Leah

The doctors couldn't tell me if I'd be in the hospital for the rest of my pregnancy, or how long they expected to delay birth. They said we would have to take it day by day.

⟜ Nina

Lying in a hospital bed for weeks, perhaps months, is not only confining physically, but also emotionally. Those who have survived hospital bed rest report a multitude of difficulties, including an inability to concentrate on simple tasks, such as reading or playing cards. This can make passing the hours quite difficult.

Relying on doctors and nurses can make you feel powerless. You may feel like you have lost all control of your life and your body. Your mate may feel left out and frustrated because there is little he can do to help you and the baby. Many strangers enter into your private lives, and, although you both know help is needed, the lack of privacy can sometimes be maddening.

The most difficult part of hospital bed rest for many women is being separated from family. Some days can be tougher than others. During the better days, you may feel good that you're doing everything you can to sustain your pregnancy. On the worst days, you may feel incredibly isolated and sad, wishing it were all over.

Recognizing that hospital bed rest is one of the most difficult obstacles you've faced in life, the following suggestions can help make your days in waiting a little easier. Chapter 9, Coming to Terms with Confinement, discusses common feelings and ways to cope.

Accept a Helping Hand

If you haven't already tapped into all your resources for help, do so now. Make a list of everyone who may offer some assistance, as well as those who might provide some solutions, such as your clergy leader or state's department of social services. Be creative. Is your neighbor the leader of a Girl Scout troop? Then perhaps she knows some responsible girls who could watch your child or walk your dog. Are there any sisterhoods or brotherhoods who do community service projects, such as preparing meals for the home-bound?

Asking for and accepting help not only benefits you and your unborn child, but also your partner who is currently overburdened with anxiety and responsibility. Your baby's siblings can use some extra attention and love, too. If you won't seek help for yourself, do it for them. (If you need financial assistance with rooming for out-of-town visitors, paying for parking, or making long-distance telephone calls, consult the hospital's social worker.)

Create a Home Away from Home

It was not home, but I was as comfortable as I could be under the circumstances.

⌒ Nina

Dr. Judith A. Maloni, a nurse who has worked with hundreds of women on hospital bed rest, suggests turning your hospital bed into a "mission control on an egg crate." First, make sure you lie on a comfortable surface, such as an egg-crate mattress (about $30 at a discount store, or check to see if your insurance will cover it), or an air mattress with a pump. Then, like the buttons and switches at NASA mission control, place everything you need in arm's reach: telephone, telephone book, TV remote control, call bell, tape recorder, clock radio, reading glasses, tissues, snacks, and any other items you want on hand.

Items from home, such as your favorite pillow, can make your mission control homey and provide some comfort and security. Nina's husband brought in their portable CD player with favorite jazz CDs, so Nina could listen to music throughout her days. Some women even bring in a portable refrigerator or a small cooler for snacks. If the hospital doesn't have a VCR/DVD to lend, consider bringing in one from home (labeled with your name).

You can add some color to those sterile walls by posting your children's drawings or schoolwork, travel or sports posters, and family or vacation photographs. Also, bring the outdoors inside with a potted plant or some flowers on your windowsill. You may enjoy watching potted tulip bulbs grow as the days go by.

Keep Up Appearances

In the hospital, I only got my hair washed once a week. I had it in a ponytail or barrettes most of the time. It looked really bad, and I even found mats in it once.

One day, my husband brought in a picture of our family for my bedside table. My hair was styled, the way I usually wear it. When the nurses saw the picture, they looked at it, then at me, and asked, "Is that really you in that photo?"

                ⌒ Leah

Wearing a hospital gown every day can make you feel and look sick. If possible, get dressed each morning. Changing between daytime and nighttime clothes can also make your days feel more normal and give you a sense of control.

Choose maternity or loose-fitting clothes, like a sweat suit, that won't interfere with medical equipment. If you haven't had time to purchase maternity wear, borrow some, ask one of your helpers to shop for your size at a consignment store, or order items through catalogs or on the Web (see Who Can Help at the end of chapter 3).

Some hospitals have beauty shops; ask if a hair stylist can come to your room. Or a family member or a close friend can fix your hair and do your nails and makeup.

Don't forget, too, that nurses aren't the only ones who can help you brush your hair, bathe, or escort you to the bathroom. Your partner, a family member, or a close friend can be taught to provide assistance. Helping you will make loved ones feel more helpful and in control.

Communicate with Caregivers

The entire time I was hospitalized I felt sheepish about bothering the nurses when I needed something. I felt like there were women there to have babies, and I was just there for observation and not very important.

⌒ Nina

It's hard to let someone care for you when you don't feel sick. But your health care is important—for both you and your baby. Share your feelings and concerns with caregivers, and never be afraid to ask questions about your care.

When you're not feeling well, or you're groggy from medication, your partner's communication with your health-care team can be valuable. He can voice opinions and concerns and ask questions. If he misses a doctor or specialist's visit, he can arrange for a telephone conference.

Remember, it is your right and your partner's right to have information pertaining to your pregnancy and baby.

Stay Connected

I just wanted to hold my twenty-month-old and kiss my husband and not feel like I wasn't allowed. I am a private person and since I was on bed rest in a teaching hospital, many people just walked in on us all the time.

⟋ Jackie

Being apart and trying to cope with a high-risk pregnancy can strain even the strongest relationships. Two-way communication—expressing how you feel and listening to each other—is critical.

Finding time together, alone, in your hospital room can also help.

If your health is stable, post a do-not-disturb sign on your door. Most hospitals provide cots or lounge chairs for loved ones to spend the night. If you have other children at home, consider arranging overnight childcare for one night a week. Many couples have date nights at least once a week, sharing takeout food and watching a video.

If you have other children, you'll need to be creative to stay connected with them, too. One mother on bed rest for five weeks was allowed to have a playpen in her hospital room when her fifteen-month-old daughter visited. Though this may be against hospital policy, or may be too stressful for you, frequent visits from children should be encouraged.

For times of separation, schedule regular telephone calls, such as before bedtime and first thing in the morning. A calendar can help your child track your time away. Some families design personalized calendars on the computer, or your family can decorate a blank craft-store calendar with drawings and photos.

Many mothers record special messages or favorite stories on audiocassettes for their children to listen to during separations. Sharing photographs is another good idea. One mother had her husband take a Polaroid snapshot of her to her son at home every day she was in the hospital; dad returned with one of their son the next morning. For more ideas on helping your partner and children cope with bed rest, see chapter 7, Your Partner's Part, and chapter 8, Siblings in Waiting.

Manage Your Visitors

Visits from friends and family can be a great way to pass the time, but too many guests, or poorly timed visits, can be burdensome. In some cases, too much stimulation may even cause contractions or high blood pressure.

> *I had a very hard time relaxing when my kids or anyone other than my husband visited me in the hospital. I was so afraid that my kids would get hurt on something, or they would make too much noise. When visitors came, they all seemed so loud and so high energy that I would get over-stimulated and agitated.*
>
> ⌐ Erin

To cut back on surprise guests, set up regular visiting hours at times that are convenient for you. Let family and friends know when to stop by, and post visiting hours on your door. Ask the nurses to enforce your wishes.

If a guest drops by and you're not up to chatting, tell him or her you are feeling too tired to talk. If you're afraid of hurting feelings, you can prearrange a way to notify your nurse that you want to be alone by using a hand signal or a special phrase. One mother inquired about the timing of her next medication dose to alert her nurse (she wasn't on any medication).

Too many telephone calls can also keep you from much-needed rest. When asked, most nurses will divert calls to the nurse's station, or turn off your line. Don't worry about offending callers; most people will understand your need for some R&R.

Celebrate Milestones

My water broke at twenty-five weeks; I was then hospitalized for the duration. My doctors told me that we really needed to make it to twenty-eight weeks.

As soon as I calmed down, I started planning a twenty-eight-week gestational birthday party. We ordered a cake and invited everyone to come (we had enough cake for the nurses, too). The party was really a goal to shoot for. It was a great way to feel good about how far I had made it and to break up the drudgery of being in there every day.

                                ⌒ Leah

At first, keeping track of time in the hospital may seem like a reminder of the constant monotony, but most women on bed rest say it actually helps them feel more positive and upbeat. Keep a calendar nearby and cross off each day that passes. Note any special visits, events, ultrasounds, or other milestones you're looking forward to—and celebrate each one. One woman had a friend give her a pedicure and manicure each Friday in celebration of another week gone by. Another's husband brought her flowers every Monday morning. Teri celebrated each week that passed by taking a shower with her favorite body wash.

Prepare for a Preemie

I called the neonatal intensive care unit and asked about their policies and treatment for preemies. I'd had a preemie previously, and I wanted to be prepared. I think I was also looking for some sort of control over yet another out-of-control pregnancy.

⟳ Leslie

By getting expert care in the hospital, you're increasing the likelihood that you'll carry close to term. Your doctor may set a gestational-age goal, such as thirty-seven weeks when most babies are developed enough for birth. For twins, the average gestation period is about two to three weeks shorter than it is for singletons. And for triplets, the gestation period is typically even shorter.

Depending on your health and your baby's gestational age, you may be spending your days in waiting in a hospital with a more advanced nursery. If your baby is born too soon, this prevents having to transport your baby to a different hospital.

There are three levels of hospital care for women who have complicated pregnancies and for babies born early. A level-I hospital, or primary care facility, provides continuing care for moms and newborns with relatively minor problems. A level-II facility manages moms and newborns with slightly more serious complications. Level-III hospitals, often called tertiary care centers, provide advanced care for women and infants with more serious complications. Level-III hospitals typically have fully equipped neonatal intensive care units (NICUs) for infants born before thirty-two weeks' gestation or with very low birth weights.

If your doctor anticipates that your baby will be born prematurely, learning about the NICU and your baby's possible health concerns can lessen some anxiety.

> *I was glad I'd already seen what a thirty-two-week baby looked like and knew what most of the medical equipment did before my baby's birth. It would have been even more shocking if I'd had to deal with my baby's premature birth and the NICU at the same time.*
>
> — Allison

Some mothers say that by visiting the NICU and seeing the preemies, they coped better with the difficulties of bed rest.

> *When I got a steroid shot, I pictured my little one breathing without a respirator because of the shots. I think I was able to endure a lot more because of the NICU images.*
>
> — Erin

If possible, you may want to visit the NICU several times during your hospitalization. Get to know the neonatalogists (doctors who specialize in preemies) and the nurses. Ask questions. Learn what you can do as a parent should your baby need special care.

Some parents find it helpful to talk with parents of a preemie who can share their experience. Ask the hospital social worker or a NICU nurse for a referral.

If your health prevents a trip to the NICU, your partner or a family member can visit and return with information. Having grandparents visit the nursery, or attend a class for preemie parents, can also help them prepare for the possibility of a grandchild born premature.

A meeting with a neonatal nurse or neonatologist may also be helpful. Your hospital may offer videos, pamphlets, or books to prepare parents for an early arrival (but only learn as much as you want to know; some information may cause unnecessary worry). Ask a nurse, a social worker, or your hospital librarian for resources. Also see Premature Birth in appendix D.

Seek Support

Undoubtedly, there will be days during your hospitalization when you feel unbearably sad, lonely, angry, and bored.

Panic began to creep in when two weeks had passed. My condition was fairly stable, and I began to notice things around me. The pink walls. The windows that didn't open. The whoosh-ching-ching of the pump that filled the air mattress under me. The nurses who came in and out at all hours to stick, poke, and monitor me. The menu that never changed. The infrequent visitors who came and then left. Everyone kept leaving but me.

⁓ Mary

These are the days when you must be willing to reach out to others. Talk about your feelings to anyone you feel comfortable with: your partner, a favorite nurse, your doctor, a close friend, a clergy person, the hospital social worker, another mom on bed rest in the hospital, or a bed-rest veteran. If you haven't connected to a bed rest support group, do so now (see Bed Rest/Support in appendix D).

Journaling is another good way to release pent-up feelings. Some women talk to God or pray. Whatever works for you is okay. Chapter 9, Coming to Terms with Confinement, offers more coping suggestions.

You may even find your own unique way of dealing with bed rest, as Leah did. She worked through her depression by focusing on the not-so-bad aspects of being in the hospital.

The depression from a bad situation and from the day-to-day monotony can be the worst enemy of a long, hospitalized pregnancy. Right away, I started talking about what I was grateful for. I found the smallest things to be thankful for, like there was a McDonald's in the hospital.

⟶ Leah

CHAPTER FIVE

Healthy Horizontal Eating

Most expectant mothers wonder how their pregnancy and changing their diet to meet new nutritional needs will affect their bodies. Some worry about gaining enough weight; others fret about gaining too much weight. Bed rest and its accompanying lifestyle change—going from an active person to an immobile one—also create concerns. You may wonder how eliminating exercise will affect your body and health.

Research shows inactivity during your pregnancy may indeed lead to some side effects. Dr. Judith A. Maloni, who has studied the effects of bed rest for over a decade, says, "During bed rest, muscles weaken, energy is depleted, weight and muscle tissue are lost, and the cardiovascular system is weakened." The longer and stricter the bed-rest sentence, the more likely you'll experience some of these influences and the longer it may take you to recover. (Recovering from bed rest is discussed later in chapter 10.)

On a more positive note, there are some specific steps you can take to slow down the impacts of immobility. Proper nutrition, discussed in this chapter, and light, doctor-approved exercises, discussed in the next chapter, can help. Taking steps to take care of yourself can also make you feel better during such a stressful time. Perhaps more importantly, taking care of yourself means you're also taking care of your baby.

WHY YOU SHOULD WATCH WHAT YOU EAT

Bridget Swinney, a registered dietitian and author of *Eating Expectantly: A Practical and Tasty Guide to Prenatal Nutrition*, says it's especially important for women on bed rest to eat well. "If you're on bed rest and at increased risk for delivering early, you may have less time to grow your baby to optimum size," says Swinney, who endured eleven weeks of bed rest while carrying her second son. She adds that women on bed rest who are carrying multiples also require "super nutrition," extra nutrition to grow more than one baby.

Of course, anyone who has been on bed rest knows that eating well while horizontal can be hard. After all, you must rely on others to buy groceries and make meals. Often these are people who are unfamiliar with your food preferences or with pregnancy nutrition.

I found it hard to be picky about what I was eating when someone else was preparing the food. They would ask, What do you want? And I would answer, Whatever there is. I didn't know what was in the cupboards or the refrigerator. Sometimes, I daydreamed about just standing in front of the opened refrigerator and checking out all the foods before choosing what I wanted.

Even when I had a stranger come in to help, I still felt guilty for asking her to bring me a snack or a drink. I was doing what was right for my baby, yet I had this nagging feeling that she thought I was lazy and that I really could wait longer for that drink.

⌒ Leah

Less activity throughout your day and sadness about your situation may also weaken your appetite. On the other hand, you may eat too much out of boredom, or after watching all those fast-food TV commercials. Physical symptoms, such as heartburn, and medical problems, such as gestational diabetes, can certainly make eating difficult as well.

I had gestational diabetes and could barely control my sugars. In fact, I ended up having to cut out fruit and most carbohydrates just to get my sugars in control—and that was with insulin injections every day! It was beyond frustrating. However, the outcome was wonderful. My baby arrived healthy and strong.

⌒ Jackie

Even the logistics of eating while lying down may encourage you to skip a meal or two.

> *I can look back now and laugh when I picture myself trying to eat peas while lying on my side. They kept rolling off the spoon and into my bed! Or the time I attempted spaghetti—what a mess!*
>
> ⌒ Allison

As most women on bed rest discover, you'll need to make a conscious effort to ensure that you're eating right. A dietitian with maternal health experience can help. Check to see if your health insurance will cover a referral (if you're hospitalized, a dietitian should be assigned to you).

If your insurance won't cover a dietitian's care, consider consulting an expert on your own. Ask your doctor for a referral, or contact the American Dietetic Association (see Who Can Help at the end of this chapter) for names of experts in your area.

If you have certain complications of pregnancy that require added nutritional care (for instance, gestational diabetes, high blood pressure, or multiple babies), you're under- or overweight, you're a teen, or you're over thirty-five, you'll need to work closely with your doctor and dietitian. To complement their advice, several helpful organizations, Web sites, and books are listed at the end of this chapter as well as under Complications in Pregnancy in appendix D.

You should also read at least one of the pregnancy nutrition books listed at the end of this chapter (after all, you have plenty of time on your hands!), and peruse the Web or some cookbooks for meal ideas. Though you probably won't do the actual cooking, you can write shopping lists, create meal plans, and even suggest recipes to your bed-rest helpers.

The remaining sections in this chapter will help you eat well during your bed-rest pregnancy.

What to Eat While Lying Low

Throughout my hospital stay, I thought about how everything I put into my mouth was going directly to my babies. I had ultrasounds about every three weeks, and each one showed that my twins were growing well. I was reassured and felt good about how my eating was helping them grow.

⟳ Danielle

I knew I was heading toward bed rest so I went to the grocery store and stocked up on plenty of fresh fruits, vegetables, cereal, and skim milk. Not that I ate poorly before bed rest, but I wanted to be extra sure I was eating healthy for my baby.

⟳ Jackie

Typically, expectant mothers carrying one baby need about 300 extra calories per day added to their before-pregnancy diet (about the number of calories in two slices of toast and a glass of orange juice). For the average-size woman, that's about 2,500 calories a day. To make every calorie count, try to follow the food-source and serving-size guides provided below, as recommended by the March of Dimes. Each day, try to eat:

- three to four servings of protein foods (necessary for the growth of new blood cells and body tissue);

- four to six servings of calcium-rich foods (these also support the growth of new body tissue and help build baby's bones and teeth);

- two to four servings of fruits (which provide vital vitamins and nutrients for baby's growth);

- three to five servings of vegetables (more vitamins and nutrients);

- six to eleven servings of grains, breads, and cereals (these are your body's main source of energy); and

- eight or more glasses of water or water-based beverages, such as decaffeinated coffee or decaffeinated tea (needed to support an increased blood supply, amniotic fluid, and extra tissue; some experts recommend ten to twelve glasses of water a day).

The following guide will help you eat the right amount from each food group:

Protein Foods

Meat, poultry, fish	2 ounces (about the size of your fist)
Eggs	2
Nuts	½ cup
Beans	1 cup

Calcium-Rich Foods

Milk	1 cup
Cheese	1½ ounces
Yogurt	1 cup
Broccoli	2 cups

Fruits

Apple, banana, orange	1 medium
Orange juice	4 ounces
Strawberries	¾ cup

Vegetables

Raw, leafy vegetables	1 cup
Cauliflower, carrots, etc.	½ cup cooked or raw

Grains, Breads, and Cereal

Bread	1 slice
Cereal, Hot	½ cup cooked
Cereal, Cold	1 cup
Rice	½ cup cooked
Pasta	½ cup cooked
Crackers	4
Tortilla	1
Bagel	1 small, ½ large
Waffle	1 medium

If you're expecting twins or more, you need to add about an extra serving of each food group to your diet (you may need less or more servings depending on your weight gain). Multiple babies often arrive two or three weeks earlier than singleton babies, so you need to eat right and gain weight as early into your pregnancy as possible. For more information on giving your multiple babies optimal nutrition, refer to Recommended Reading at the end of this chapter and Multiples/Publications in appendix D.

By eating a wide variety of foods from each food group in the appropriate amounts, and by taking a daily prenatal vitamin as recommended by your physician, you'll be following a healthy pregnancy diet. In addition, you should pay special attention to getting enough of the nutrients discussed below.

Folic Acid

Low levels of the B-vitamin folic acid, especially prior to pregnancy and during the first trimester, have been associated with birth defects of the brain and spinal cord. Therefore, folic acid should be an essential part of your diet throughout your pregnancy. Folic acid plays an important role in making new cells, and research shows that a pregnant woman's folic acid and iron intake can increase a baby's weight and length.

The Institute of Medicine recommends that expectant women consume 600 micrograms of folic acid each day. Two eight-ounce glasses of orange juice has about 200 micrograms of folic acid. A multivitamin or folic-acid supplement, approved by your doctor, can provide you with about 400 micrograms. You should also eat foods rich in folic acid, such as fortified breads, asparagus, leafy green vegetables, broccoli, peanuts, peas, and beans. Since folic acid is water-soluble, cook foods in as little water and for the shortest time as possible to retain nutrients.

A Word of Caution

Only take supplemental vitamins and minerals that are recommended by your doctor or dietitian. Taking too much of some vitamins and minerals can actually do more harm than good.

Iron

Your blood volume increases up to 50 percent during pregnancy, causing you to need two times as much iron. Fortunately, Mother Nature comes to the rescue by helping pregnant women absorb two times as much iron in the food they consume.

The best sources of iron come from animals: meat and eggs. Other good iron-rich foods are highly fortified breakfast cereals, such as Product 19 or Total, fortified oatmeal, apricots, raisins, and spinach.

Consuming a beverage or food high in vitamin C (orange or grape juice, watermelon, tomatoes, and potatoes) with iron-rich foods can also increase the amount of iron your body absorbs. Stay away from beverages with caffeine, such as tea and coffee, as these are iron inhibitors and can significantly decrease iron absorption.

Your doctor may also recommend a prenatal vitamin with added iron or an iron supplement, especially if you show signs of iron-deficiency anemia (a lack of red blood cells that carry oxygen through the blood), or you're carrying multiples. Research has shown that anemia may increase the risk of delivering a low-birth-weight or premature baby, and the National Academy of Sciences now recommends that all pregnant women take an iron supplement.

Calcium

Most dietitians recommend that pregnant women consume about 50 percent more calcium (about 1,200 micrograms daily) than is typically recommended for women over twenty-five. Where does all that extra calcium go? Into your baby's bones.

Some early research indicated that supplemental calcium during pregnancy helps lower blood pressure and reduce the risk of pre-eclampsia (high blood pressure occurring only in pregnancy). A 1997 study proved otherwise. But many physicians familiar with this new research continue to recommend added calcium for high-risk pregnancies.

Three or more servings of milk or other dairy products should do the trick. If you're lactose intolerant, a variety of low-lactose and reduced-lactose products are available, and you can ask your doctor about taking a calcium supplement.

Zinc

Zinc promotes growth of body tissue and bones. A deficiency in zinc has been linked to low birth weight, increased pregnancy complications, and premature birth. You can get zinc from turkey, lean pork, shrimp, whole grains, and almonds.

Essential Fatty Acids

Some essential fatty acids, such as omega-3 oils found in fish, are important for a baby's brain development and for the growth of nerves and eye tissue (retinas). Try to include fish, such as salmon, tuna, trout, anchovies, and mackerel, in your diet. Tuna snack packs can be handy (but, see limitations below).

Some fish should be avoided or consumed in moderation during pregnancy because of mercury contamination that may affect brain and nervous system development. Experts advise eating shark and swordfish no more than once a month, and don't eat those tuna snack packs more than two times a week.

Other sources of omega-3 fats include canola, flaxseed, and soybean oil, as well as Eggland's Best Eggs.

Vitamin D

Some experts believe that women on bed rest, with little or no exposure to the sun, may not make enough vitamin D. Consult your doctor or dietitian about consuming additional vitamin D. Milk and prenatal vitamins are fortified with this important vitamin.

MEAL PLANNING AND GROCERY SHOPPING

Plan ahead if you know you may have to go on strict bed rest. I made dinners and healthful cookies and froze them. If you don't end up needing them, you'll have some meals ready to serve after baby's homecoming.

— Jackie

A Healthy Sample Menu

Dietitian Bridget Swinney suggests that you keep a journal of the servings you eat in each food group for a few days to see how well you're eating. The following is an example of a healthy-eating day during pregnancy from the March of Dimes:

Breakfast
Orange juice
Bran flakes with peaches
Muffin or biscuit
Milk

Lunch
Vegetable juice
Egg salad on lettuce
Two slices of pumpernickel
    bread
Tomato slices

Dinner
Baked chicken
Mixed green salad
Baked sweet or white potato
Milk
Whole-wheat roll
Apple
Ice cream

Snack
Milk
Peanut butter and crackers

My children and I have food allergies, which made food preparation challenging for others. I made lists of what the kids and I could eat, and we never had dangerous foods in the house.

⌒ Erin

Many women on bed rest find it helpful to plan at least a few large meals at the beginning of each week for others to fix. If possible, ask someone to cook several meals once a week on a regular basis. Try to pick dishes that aren't too greasy or messy and require little or no refrigeration or preparation. If you are sensitive to sodium, keep in mind that you may want to limit your consumption of canned and convenience foods, which are often high in sodium.

Keep an ongoing grocery list so you're prepared when someone offers to shop for you. Be specific about brands, sizes, and flavors. This will eliminate the time-consuming task of others having to guess your preferences. Also, provide your helper with coupons. Clipping coupons is a great way for you to help the family budget while on bed rest. See Who Can Help at the end of this chapter for Web sites that offer coupons (some even have meal-planning ideas with shopping lists and recipes).

When writing your shopping list, be sure to include healthful snacks, too. Some ideas: hard-boiled eggs, crackers and peanut butter, string cheese, bran muffins, snack-size applesauce and canned fruit, and small cans of juice. Soup in a cup, such as black bean, lentil, and couscous, is not only easy to make, but an excellent source of fiber.

You may also want to check to see if any of your local grocery stores provide food-shopping services; some may even deliver. Larger stores rent small freezers, so you can store food in the garage until someone gets home. If you live in a metropolitan area, your local grocery or drugstore may have a Web site that allows you to do the shopping through the computer; the store may then deliver, or a bed-rest helper can pick up the bags at a fulfillment center. Look under "grocery shopping" in your favorite search engine, and see Who Can Help at the end of this chapter.

Getting the Most Out of Meals

I had to be extremely careful about bending over during those rare occasions when I got up. So, if I dropped any food on the floor, it stayed there until my husband came home. It made me wish we had a dog!

— Barb

To make dining in bed easier, try these ideas from bed-rest veterans:

- Fill your nightstand drawer or a basket by the couch full of snacks (fruit cups, low-fat cookies, canned juices, a jar of peanut butter, graham crackers, wheat crackers, and a few treats).

- When you get tired of water, add a slice of lemon or try some flavored waters.

- A bath towel thrown over your body and under your chin will keep the food crumbs out of bed. A bib can save clothes from messy drips.

- Keep a supply of bendable straws and paper plates on hand.

- Use a thermos for soups and milkshakes. An ice chest and a cooler with frozen ice packs are great for milk, cottage cheese, sandwiches, tossed salad with a bottle of dressing, and frozen "gogurts" (yogurt in a tube).

- To keep drinks and yogurts cold and to prevent spoilage, freeze during the night, remove in the morning, and enjoy when they defrost.

- When eating takeout, good choices are barbecued or roasted chicken, Chinese or Japanese food, and bean burritos.

- If you don't have a crock pot, borrow or buy one now. It's the simplest way for your partner or helpers to prepare healthful, easy meals. Check out some of the great crock-pot cooking Web sites and crock-pot cookbooks, too.

HOSPITAL FOOD: THE GOOD, THE BAD, AND THE UGLY

One of my favorite things about being on hospital bed rest was the full meals that were delivered. After at-home bed rest, I thought it was the best thing in the world that I didn't have to ask anyone to prepare my meals—they just showed up on time!

I bragged and bragged about how good the hospital food was. I know people thought I was crazy, but my eating was so important for my baby. I not only ate full hospital meals, but also a glass of whole milk and an Ensure with every meal. I knew that everything I ate would give my baby a better chance.

⌒ Leah

When I was in the hospital, my husband would visit me every day during his lunch hour so we could eat lunch together.

⌒ Teri

After you've been in the hospital for a while, you catch on to how to get what you really want. For instance, the hospital didn't have decaf ice tea, so I'd order two hot decaf teas and a big glass of ice.

⌒ Jackie

Eating well in the hospital can be easier than eating well at home: A menu is delivered to your room each day (usually with nutritional guidelines), you don't have to worry about who will prepare your meals, and you even know the approximate time you'll be served. If you're diabetic, you'll receive a special menu, and you can pick from a variety of foods. As one diabetic mom-to-be says, "I really enjoyed not having to measure or count. I could eat whatever came on my tray!"

Of course, the food provided may not always be to your liking, and eating in bed, often alone, can get old fast. As Jackie says, "I didn't need a calendar; I knew what day it was by the hospital menu. So did my hubby. He would come in and say, 'Oh, seafood casserole. It must be Thursday!' "

Hospital menus typically run on a two-week cycle, so, if you're on long-term bed rest, food selections will become repetitive. But at least you'll know which days to order out!

To make the most out of hospital dining, try these ideas tested by bed-rest veterans:

- Don't be afraid to speak up if the food served tastes terrible, is not cooked well, or is too cold. The nurses know you're eating for two (or perhaps more), and they should help you get an edible replacement meal.

- If you really dislike a lot of the hospital food, or you're really bored by the choices, consult a dietitian about alternatives, or ask your doctor to request special foods for you.

- Ask if there is a refrigerator nearby where you can keep a few favorite foods, such as yogurt or ice cream. Store favorite nonperishable snacks in your bedside table.

- Check with local restaurants to see if any will deliver to the hospital, or have a friend or a family member pick up your order on the way for a visit.

- When visitors ask what they can bring you, don't be shy about specifying foods you're craving. It made one mother's day when her friend brought her fresh mangos.

- For variety, ask the nurses if you can order food that isn't on the regular menu, such as a sandwich or a salad, from the cafeteria or other in-hospital restaurant. You can have a friend or a family member check out the cafeteria choices for ideas.

- Don't be afraid to request more than one item on the menu. For example, ask for two glasses of orange juice.

- If a visitor you'd like to eat with won't be arriving until after a meal is served, ask if the food can be kept warm or in a refrigerator until your friend arrives.

NUTRITIONAL AIDS FOR COMMON COMPLAINTS

Some common pregnancy complaints can be intensified when you're spending most or all of your time in a horizontal position. You should discuss any discomfort or concerns with your doctor or dietitian. In some cases, a simple change in your positioning or diet can make a big difference.

Discussed next are the common concerns of women on bed rest and suggestions for nutritional cures.

Low Weight Gain

I lost about eight pounds around my twenty-fourth week of pregnancy bed rest and never gained during the next five weeks. But the twins were a good birth weight for their gestational age.

⌒ Danielle

By doing so little throughout your day, you may think those unused calories are going to add up. So, it may be a surprise if the scale actually goes down. "Current evidence indicates that weight loss is a side effect of bed rest for some women, but it doesn't seem to affect infant birth weight," says Dr. Maloni.

Experts believe weight loss during bed rest is caused by loss of fluid, bone, and muscle. Some believe medicine to prevent preterm labor may also burn calories. A poor appetite caused by medications, discomfort from heartburn or constipation, and sadness about your situation may also play a part.

If you're having trouble eating, try to choose foods that give the most nutrition for calories (eggs, milk, and yogurt), and ask your doctor about taking a calcium supplement. Dried fruit is also a good source of concentrated healthful calories. If you're expecting multiples, your dietitian may recommend a high-calorie food supplement, such as Ensure, or adding an instant breakfast mix to milk. Because multiples often arrive before term, dietitians recommend that women carrying more than one baby gain weight early in the pregnancy.

In addition, try to drink fluids between meals, rather than during meals, and stick to regular eating times. You may also find it easier to eat five or six small meals, rather than three large ones. Eating may be more enjoyable, too, if you eat with visitors.

Any significant weight loss or consistent lack of weight gain should be discussed with your doctor. An evaluation can be done to ensure that your baby is growing at the proper rate for gestational age.

High Weight Gain

Overeating because "it's something to do" and little if any exercise causes some women to gain too much weight during bed rest. If this is your concern, try eating more low-calorie foods that are rich in nutrients. Some suggestions: raw vegetables, fruit, celery and peanut butter, unbuttered popcorn, skim or nonfat milk, popcorn cakes, and low-fat yogurt. Stick to regular meal times and less snacking in between (but don't deprive yourself, or you may binge later). Ask your food-preparation helpers to cut back on fats and nonnutritious desserts. If friends bring goodies, freeze them to avoid eating them all at once.

If you notice a sudden weight gain (three or more pounds in a week) and/or swelling in your hands, feet, or face, contact your doctor immediately. It could be a sign of pregnancy-induced high blood pressure, or preeclampsia (a serious condition characterized by sudden weight gain, high blood pressure, and protein in the urine).

Nausea and Vomiting

To reduce nausea, never go for long periods without food, and try to eat five or six small meals a day. Drink fluids between but not with meals. Stick to lightly seasoned foods and avoid spicy dishes. When you feel nauseated, take small sips of apple juice or a carbonated beverage, such as ginger ale, or nibble on a dry cracker. Also, avoid offensive odors, such as smoke, and get some fresh air (have someone open a window by your bed).

If nausea or vomiting persists, consult your doctor. There are several nonprescription and prescription medicines that may help.

Heartburn

A burning sensation in the chest, heartburn, is a common problem of pregnancy and can be accentuated by a reclined position. To relieve heartburn, try eating five or six smaller meals throughout the day, eat slowly, and chew adequately. If allowed, sitting up with pillows propped behind you, or raising the head of your bed, may help. Ask your doctor about taking an antacid.

Constipation

I always ordered lots of veggies in the hospital. I was afraid
of getting constipated during bed rest. I asked for prune juice
too, even though it was the consistency of motor oil!

⌒ Jackie

Being on bed rest may prevent regular bowel activity. You need to be careful about straining and pushing, which could lead to painful hemorrhoids (varicose veins in the rectal area that protrude and cause itching and discomfort). In some cases, straining and pushing during a bowel movement can induce early labor.

Whole grains (bran and wheat germ) are foods that encourage bowel movements without straining. You can also try drinking more juice and water and eating more fruits, vegetables, and foods with fiber. Easy-to-eat fiber foods include snack packs of carrots, fresh fruit, and dried fruit. Hot water with a teaspoon of lemon juice may also help.

Dietitian Bridget Swinney gives this advice: "Start every morning with a high-fiber cereal and fruit, such as bran flakes with fresh blueberries, strawberries, or raisins. Eat four or more servings of whole-grain foods, such as whole-wheat bread, crackers, or pasta, the rest of the day. Eat six or more fresh fruits and vegetables every day and drink plenty of water. This should keep constipation at bay."

Baby Pick-Me-Up
A High-Energy Drink

(2 SERVINGS)

1 frozen or ½ cup canned peaches or nectarines (freeze for 45 minutes or more)

½ banana

½ cup frozen strawberries

1 cup low-fat vanilla yogurt or 1 cup milk plus sweetener to taste

2 tablespoons nonfat dry milk

Combine all ingredients in blender. Makes approximately 2 cups. If you don't have frozen fruit, adding ice to desired consistency will increase the volume.

Nutrient analysis per serving: 274 calories ▪ 8 grams protein ▪ 6 grams fiber ▪ 2 grams fat

(Reprinted with permission from Eating Expectantly by Bridget Swinney, M.S., R.N., Meadowbrook Press, 2000)

If the problem persists, ask your doctor about stool softeners or mild laxatives.

Fatigue

Lying in bed all day is *not* restful: It interrupts your sleep-wake cycle, making you feel tired. You may also feel overtired because of the stress you're under and from boredom. Fatigue can also be caused by insufficient iron in the blood (anemia); therefore, you should report any unusual fatigue to your doctor. Also, make sure you're eating lots of iron-rich foods. And eat snacks high in protein and carbohydrates but low in sugar (see recipe on page 93) to avoid dramatic changes in blood sugar, which can increase fatigue.

Leg and Muscle Cramps

Leg and muscle cramps are a common pregnancy complaint. Experts believe a lack of calcium, or ratio of calcium to another mineral, can cause cramping. Cramps may be more common in women on bed rest because lack of activity can decrease calcium in the bones. Dehydration and low levels of potassium in the body have also been linked to cramping.

Ask your doctor about changing your calcium intake. Make sure you eat plenty of calcium-rich foods and those with potassium (bananas, orange juice, and potatoes are good sources). Increase your liquids, too.

ADDITIONAL FOOD FOR THOUGHT

I had a hard time at first accepting all the help, but after a while I realized it was completely necessary. In truth, I really didn't have the energy to bother with healthful food choices, but my family and friends did. In the end, I was really thankful that people helped me.

⌒ Sara

My mother-in-law cooked and followed my diabetic diet to a T. She even looked for special diabetic foods so that I could have some treats, like sugar-free cookies. That made bed rest and eating better.

⌒ Jackie

One day a neighborhood mom came by with her own muffin pan and all the necessary ingredients. She knew I'd enjoy her muffins more if they came straight from the oven!

⌒ Nina

This chapter discussed why eating well during bed rest is so important for you and your baby, giving you one more reason to accept a helping hand (or two or three!). Chapter 2 provides ideas for finding volunteers. You can also check with local religious and non-profit groups, such as Meals on Wheels, to see if they can help. Sometimes, all it takes is a phone call.

Of course, food is one of the first things most of us think to offer in a time of need. So, once people learn you're confined to bed, you'll probably have more than enough home-cooked meals show up at your door. One woman on bed rest said her friends threw her a "casserole shower." She had enough casseroles to cover dinners during bed rest—and the first two weeks after her baby was home.

WHO CAN HELP

American Dietetic Association
216 W. Jackson Blvd.
Chicago, IL 60606
(312) 899-0040
(800) 366-1655 (consumer nutrition hot line)
www.eatright.org

For coupons:
www.coolsavings.com
www.couponsurfer.com
www.edealfinder.com
www.mycoupons.com
www.thatscheap.com
www.valupage.com
and major grocery stores' Web sites

For easy meals:
busycooks.miningco.com
www.cyber-kitchen.com
www.mega-zine.com/kitchen/crock-pot/

www.minutemeals.com

www.quickneasyrecipes.com

For grocery delivery:

www.netgrocer.com

www.peapod.com

www.webvan.com

For meal planning:

www.bettycrocker.com/planner

www.bhglive.com/food/planner.html

www.cooking.com/recipes/reweekmp.asp

www.mealsforyou.com

www.my-meals.com

For restaurant service:

www.food.com

RECOMMENDED READING

Also see Multiples/Publications in appendix D.

Am I Glowing Yet? Understanding and Coping with the Common and Not-So-Common Miseries of Pregnancy by Virginia Hege Tobiassen (Chicago Review Press, 1995) (out of print; check your library or used bookstore)

Eating Expectantly: A Practical and Tasty Guide to Prenatal Nutrition, 3rd ed., by Bridget Swinney, M.S., R.D. (Meadowbrook Press, 2000); www.healthyfoodzone.com

Nutrition and Pregnancy: A Complete Guide from Preconception to Postdelivery by Judith E. Brown, R.D., M.P.H., Ph.D. (Lowell House, 1998)

Nutrition for a Healthy Pregnancy by Elizabeth Somer, M.A., R.D. (Henry Holt, 1995)

The Pregnancy Cookbook by Hope Ricciotti, M.D. (W. W. Norton and Co., 1996)

The Vegetarian Mother and Baby Book by Rose Elliot (Pantheon Books, 1997)

CHAPTER SIX

Couch Calisthenics

Throughout my bed-rest term, it never occurred to me to ask my doctor about exercise. After all, if he prescribed staying off my feet to ward off early delivery, shouldn't I avoid any extra activity? Not necessarily, say the experts. In fact, light, doctor-approved exercises can be quite beneficial for the mom-to-be on bed rest—both physically and mentally.

Before we go any further, though, let me stress the importance of discussing any physical activity with your doctor. Each pregnancy is unique and can vary from day to day. Only your health-care provider and you can evaluate your ability to exercise. Call your doctor, or take this book with you on your next appointment, and get clear instructions for what you can and cannot do. Also, keep your doctor informed of any changes during your pregnancy.

With that said, let's now talk about how bed rest and its accompanying lack of activity may affect you.

THE EFFECTS OF LYING LOW

Limited or no activity is not natural for the body. Among other benefits, exercise helps blood to circulate and muscles and bones to stay strong. When you become immobile, even for a short time, your body is affected by this change. You may begin to feel adverse effects, such as muscle weakness and dizziness.

> *During my first bed-rest pregnancy, I suffered muscle atrophy and damaged nerves in my back and hips. I also experienced burning sensations down my leg and into my feet for nearly a year afterward. I was on bed rest longer during my second pregnancy, but benefited from lessons learned. I used a different bed and had physical therapy, and I didn't suffer any nerve damage.*
>
> — Kendra

Research on how bed rest physically affects pregnant women is minimal. However, there is much research on the effects of bed rest in women (and men) who are not pregnant, thanks to the advent of the space age. Wanting to know how weightlessness in space affects astronauts, scientists confined people to bed for prolonged periods to identify the impacts of activity restriction. Researchers also performed extensive studies on astronauts during space missions to see if exercise lessens immobility's influences.

What the studies found was that bed rest, or lack of weight-bearing exercise, causes numerous changes in every system of the body. When standing is infrequent, body fluids shift from the legs to the upper body and head, and can subsequently affect circulation, heart rate, metabolism, and digestion. Disuse of muscles can lead to atrophy (a wasting away of tissue), and decreased weight bearing with accompanying calcium loss can weaken bones. In addition, this research shows that exercise that does not involve weight resistance does little to counteract these adverse results (though it can relieve some associated discomfort).

Expectant women on bed rest often experience similar side effects. In "Antepartum Bed Rest: Case Studies, Research, and Nursing Care" (Association of Women's Health, Obstetric and Neonatal Nurses, 1998), Dr. Judith A. Maloni identifies the adverse physical symptoms of bed rest documented by research. These include muscle weakness, cardiovascular deconditioning, fatigue, backache, muscle ache, joint pain, difficulty concentrating, dizziness, shortness of breath, difficulty sleeping, and weight loss. The stricter and longer the bed rest, the more likely a woman will experience some of these influences.

Now for the good news: You don't have to take these ill effects lying down (excuse the pun). If your condition permits, weight-bearing exercises, or simply getting up and walking around, can help your muscles stay strong. Isometric exercises and stretches done in bed or on the couch may relieve discomfort, stiffness, and stress. Leg and feet exercises may reduce the risk of blood clots, caused by slowed circulation. If you have gestational diabetes, light upper-arm exercises (fifteen to thirty minutes using two-pound weights) may help keep your blood glucose levels under control. Most importantly, any exercise will make you feel better.

> *In my experience, hospital patients look forward with enthusiasm to this cheerful part of their day when [a therapist visits] and they learn what they can do. The expectant mother, with spirits lifted and no longer feeling like a "failed incubator," can enjoy a program that stretches, strengthens, relaxes, and reassures. The psychological benefits are just as significant as the physical activities.*
>
> ⌒ Elizabeth Noble, physical therapist, in *Essential Exercises for the Childbearing Year*

HOW PHYSICAL THERAPY CAN HELP

Physical therapy was one of the few things I could do for myself that was a reminder of the active person I had been prior to bed rest. I feel that it helped me make a better recovery, too.

⌒ Kendra

Ideally, your health insurance will cover physical therapy or at least a consultation with a therapist. Coverage may depend on how long your doctor thinks you'll be off your feet and your prescribed level of activity restriction. If you have previous health concerns, such as knee or back problems, your insurance may cover therapy to prevent these problems from becoming worse. Consult with your doctor and health-insurance representative.

Hospitalized women should receive therapy as part of care. This may also include help from an occupational therapist, who will help you learn to function throughout the day and night in a bed-rest position.

A physical therapist (PT) will assess your joint motion, muscle strength and endurance, and your heart and lung function. Taking your high-risk pregnancy and any other concerns into account, a PT will then develop therapeutic exercises tailored to your individual abilities. A PT can also teach you the least stressful ways to sit, stand, and position yourself in bed or on the couch.

To find a PT familiar with high-risk pregnancy, ask your physician for a referral, or contact your local chapter of the American Physical Therapy Association (see Who Can Help at the end of this chapter).

EXERCISE FOR A LIMITED BED REST

How often you're allowed to get up and how long you stand and walk will greatly affect the way your body reacts to bed rest. Simply standing up, taking the longest route to the bathroom, or walking down the hospital corridor can help your blood to circulate and your muscles to stay strong.

Some doctors prescribe the "ten/fifty rule," allowing a woman to move about for ten minutes after every fifty minutes of rest (during daytime hours, of course). Though not researched, Dr. Maloni says, "If a woman can be on her feet for ten minutes each hour during every waking hour, it may offset muscle atrophy." Discuss this option with your doctor.

Your doctor may also permit you to do exercises against the resistance of a PT or with small weights. Elizabeth Noble, P.T., who founded the Obstetrics and Gynecology Section (now called the Section on Women's Health) of the American Physical Therapy Association, suggests, if you don't have some light weights available, making weights out of strong, doubled plastic bags of sand or rice (ask your doctor or PT how much weights should weigh). Fill two bags, tie the ends together, and put them on your ankles, allowing the bags to hang down on each side. Then, sitting over the side of the bed (if allowed), straighten one knee. Or, you can lie down in bed at a left tilt and raise one leg while holding it straight out. Do five repetitions per leg.

Noble also suggests using a Theraband, an elastic band that comes in different grades and colors and is available through many medical supply companies. "This flexible tubing can be hooked around the foot or side rail of your bed, a door knob, or a nearby chair to form a stirrup so you can work your hips, knees, and feet against resistance," she says.

Some doctors prescribe water therapy to reduce swelling, increase blood flow, and lower blood pressure. A 1990 article in *Obstetrics and*

Gynecology found immersion in water more effective than bed rest in treating edema.

Lisa, on modified bed rest for preeclampsia, spent one to two hours a day shoulder-deep in a pool (no swimming or horizontal floating). "I used a floating device to hold on to so I could stay vertical and not have to stand on the pool floor the whole time," she says. Not only did it reduce her edema, Lisa also found the water calming and soothing. Ask your doctor or PT if water exercise is an option for you.

The light exercises discussed in the next section are commonly recommended by PTs, but you may be permitted to do more strenuous ones depending on your condition. Again, consult your doctor or PT, and ask specifically about what is considered safe and why. You may even want to take along this book and a pregnancy fitness book and review potential exercises. Perhaps some can be modified for your individual condition.

Try to avoid lying flat on your back when exercising: The weight on the uterus can sometimes put pressure on your major blood vessels and interfere with optimal blood flow. A pillow under your right hip can put you in a left-tilt position (lying on your left side promotes optimal blood flow, but you can lie on your right side, too). Try to stay away from movements that increase pressure on your uterus. When switching sides (for example, from left to right), roll like a log keeping your head on the pillow.

Before you begin exercising, make sure you have plenty of drinking water nearby. To prevent dehydration, take small sips of water during your exercise time and a longer drink when you're finished.

Establish a regular exercise time, ideally after you use the bathroom and not right after a meal. Make your workout enjoyable and relaxing by playing some favorite music.

When you begin, start exercising slowly and take regular breaths, exhaling as you begin each movement. "Exhaling will prevent increases in pressure on your abdomen and fluctuations in circulation that occur with straining," says Noble. "I cannot emphasize enough the importance of proper breathing. Without it, you may do more harm than good."

Remember to listen to your body while exercising, and pay close attention to proper positioning, particularly as you gain weight during your pregnancy. Stop activity if you feel dizzy or lightheaded, feel any type of discomfort, become tired, or experience any of the warning signs listed on page 111.

SOME SIMPLE EXERCISES

Do each of the following exercises about six to ten times during your workout. Increase repetitions after a few days. With your doctor's approval, you may want to exercise two or three times a day.

Kegel Exercises

These strengthen the muscles of your pelvic floor, which support your baby. Lie on your left side, or sit up if allowed. Squeeze your pelvic muscles (as if you were stopping and starting urination). Try not to tighten your abdominal or buttock muscles. Hold for ten counts, then slowly release. Performing quick holds (ten repetitions of three counts each) two times a day will help strengthen your pelvic muscles, too.

Pelvic Tilts

While lying on your back at a left tilt (use a pillow under your right hip) with your knees bent, press the small of your back against the bed as you exhale.

Back Stretches

While lying on your back at a left tilt with your knees bent, press your arms into the bed while exhaling. These can be done at the same time as pelvic tilts.

Abdominal Diaphragm Breathing

Lying on your back at a left tilt with your knees bent, breathe in deeply, letting your stomach rise. If permitted, tighten the abdominal muscles as you slowly exhale through your mouth.

Curl-ups and Head Lifts

Lying on your back at a left tilt with your knees bent, place your hands on your stomach and exhale as you raise your head slowly. Keeping your back against the bed (but staying tilted), lift your head and shoulders up with your chin tucked. If this exercise is not permitted, or you have trouble doing it, you can raise your head and curl your neck to look at your stomach.

Neck Stretches

Keeping your shoulders level and relaxed, tilt your head to the right without straining; now, move your head to the left. Move your head slowly in a circular motion.

Shoulder Stretches

Raise your right shoulder to your right ear, without tilting your head. Relax, and slowly drop your shoulder. Switch sides. Roll both shoulders up and forward.

Arm Lifts

Lift one arm up slowly to the side and over your head and bring back down. Remember, exhale as you begin the exercise; inhale as you rest. Repeat with your other arm. For resistance, hold light weights or canned goods of the same weight. Arm exercises will help when it's time to carry around that newborn baby (or babies), car seat, and diaper bag!

Bicep Presses

Holding cans or two-pound weights, extend your arms in front of you at shoulder level and bend your arms at the elbows. Bring your hands to your shoulders, working your biceps.

Hand Squeezes

To build forearms, squeeze a hard rubber ball, such as a tennis ball.

Bridges

Lying on your back at a left tilt with your knees bent, raise your hips off the bed; keep your shoulders down. (If you need to use a bedpan, this is the movement you'll need to do to slide it underneath.)

Modified Leg Lifts

Lying on your back at a left tilt with one knee bent, bend your opposite knee up toward your chest. Straighten the leg by slowly kicking up toward the ceiling. Lower your knee to the bed. Repeat with your other leg. A paper plate placed under your foot will make sliding easier.

Leg Slides

Lying on your back at a left tilt with your knees bent, slowly slide your leg out. Straighten your knees while keeping your back straight. Slowly pull both knees back up.

Ankle Stretches

Move your foot up and down. Move it in a clockwise direction, then reverse. Try tracing a few letters of the alphabet. Rest your right ankle on your left knee and circle. Repeat with your left ankle on your right knee. You can also push your feet against the bed or wall.

EXERCISE FOR A STRICT BED REST

Exercising three times a day in the hospital didn't keep my calves from becoming so skinny that even the nurses gaped

A Word of Caution

Stop exercising and consult your doctor immediately if you experience any of the following symptoms:

- shortness of breath
- regular contractions
- menstrual-like or intestinal cramping
- abdominal or pelvic pain
- back pain
- excessive vaginal discharge
- bleeding

at them. However, I did find that exercise helped a little with the muscle soreness.

⁓ Leah

In my case, any exercise brought on contractions, even simple Kegels, so my doctor said absolutely no exercising. I had to just lie there for twenty-two weeks. On Christmas Day, I tried getting up, walking down the stairs, and into the living room. I thought I was going to break down and cry because of the pain.

⁓ Rachel

If you're rarely allowed to get out of bed, or not allowed at all, you will soon begin to feel the results of immobility. Research shows that atrophy can begin after only six hours of inactivity, and much muscle mass can be lost after three to seven days. With your doctor's approval, you may do all of the exercises mentioned in the last section. However, your health may warrant a no-exercise prescription.

Without weight-bearing activity, there is little you can do to prevent atrophy. However, frequent free movements of your limbs will relieve soreness and stiffness, maintain mobility, and encourage circulation. With your doctor's okay, bend your legs, stretch your arms over your head, circle your shoulders, clasp your hands in front of you, open and close your fists, point and flex your feet, and do those Kegels.

Keep in mind that once your baby arrives, you can start to get back into shape. As one mother says, "After six weeks on bed rest, my legs and arms were so weak, and I'd get out of breath after a simple trip to the bathroom. But I kept my eye on the prize—a full-term baby. And a month after my son arrived, I joined a gym."

WHO CAN HELP

American Physical Therapy Association
111 N. Fairfax St.
Alexandria, VA 22314
(800) 999-APTA ((800) 999-2782)
www.apta.org

RECOMMENDED READING

Essential Exercises for the Childbearing Year, 4th ed., by Elizabeth Noble, P.T. (New Life Images, 1995); www.elizabethnoble.com

Obstetric and Gynecological Care in Physical Therapy, 2nd ed., by Rebecca G. Stephenson, B.S., P.T., and Linda J. O'Connor, M.S., P.T. (Slack, 2000)

The Pregnancy Exercise Book by Judy Difiore (HarperCollins, 2000)

CHAPTER SEVEN

Your Partner's Part

One of a woman's biggest concerns during bed rest is how her lifestyle change will affect her partner, who must take on added responsibility during those long days in waiting.

> *During my pregnancy I was very afraid that my husband might feel as though he shouldn't have married someone who was so much trouble. I think he was more exhausted throughout the pregnancy than I was.*
>
> ⌒ Jackie

> *I felt so guilty because I was making my husband go through all this.*
>
> ⌒ Leslie

In addition, though you may not realize it, you may worry about how your partner will react to the changes bed rest causes and how your relationship might be affected. In some cases, relationships and feelings between couples do change. But, in most cases, concerns about your partner's reactions are grounded in how you are feeling about being sentenced to bed—and not how your partner is truly feeling. Certainly a high-risk pregnancy and accompanying bed-rest prescription impact partnerships and conflict and disappointment can occur. But, for the most part, effects on relationships are positive, often deepening your love and respect for one another.

> *My husband and I learned so much about each other from our first bed-rest experience. We used this knowledge during our second bed rest and survived much better. We learned how to communicate more effectively. We learned that there are times when it is better to have outside support than to rely on just each other. Our bed-rest experiences gave us the opportunity to become better partners.*
>
> ⌒ Erin

This chapter will affirm that your concerns regarding your partner are a normal part of pregnancy bed rest. It will also help you understand the common feelings of men affected by bed rest, as well as provide some solutions for keeping your relationship intact. By sharing these with your loved one, you can work together to make bed rest a more positive experience.

HIS SIDE OF THE BED

In most cases, as soon as mom hits the covers, dad takes over his partner's role in addition to his usual responsibilities. This typically includes more household duties and child care, along with caring for his mate's needs. Before going off to work, he may need to make mom's meals or pack a bag for a later hospital visit. If there are other children, he may need to get them ready for day care or school. Once at work, concern about the well-being of both his unborn baby and his partner, as well as financial stresses, may make it difficult for him to concentrate.

> *It was tough trying to keep up with work. Even though my supervisors were very understanding, I knew I wasn't performing the way I should. I always felt as if I should be somewhere else, at the hospital, at work, with our two-year-old, and my mental focus wasn't there. The worst was not having enough time to do more with my daughter.*
>
> — Michael

A father is often torn by how best to support his family during bed rest. Should he be the breadwinner, the housekeeper, the caregiver, or the jack-of-all-trades? "If dad previously felt competent about his role in the family, bed rest can be especially challenging," says psychologist Mara Stein. "Suddenly, he is pulled in many directions, and he is faced with demands in areas in which he may not feel especially skilled."

> *I felt guilty because I was working so much, but, when I was home, I felt guilty because I thought I should be working since I was now the primary breadwinner. It was a conflicting time. I was completely torn.*
>
> ⌒ Kevin

In addition, just as women sometimes attribute a complicated pregnancy to something they may have done, so do some men. An expectant dad may blame himself for impregnating his wife and putting her health in jeopardy. He may feel guilty about not being more excited about the baby or for leaving his wife alone during work hours.

> *I still have a lot of guilt because I wasn't more supportive of Leslie during bed rest. I'd just started a new job and, when my boss quit, I had to do my boss's job and my job.*
>
> ⌒ Kevin

Many men feel helpless and powerless during a high-risk pregnancy because they can't "fix" things. Anxiety about the outcome of his partner and baby as well as feelings of self-blame, inadequacy, and powerlessness can be overwhelming at times.

If a couple has previously faced a complicated pregnancy or birth, it may be difficult for them to separate this pregnancy from that one. This can be an incredibly frightening time for both parents. Talking about feelings, with each other and with others, can be especially helpful.

> *With our first pregnancy, we lost quadruplets after a short bed rest. With this pregnancy, my wife was in bed for over six months. Almost every night I woke up to check on her. I was so scared she'd go into preterm labor and we'd have to rush to the hospital. To others, I probably appeared pretty calm. But internally, I was sweating bullets.*
>
> ⌒ Matt

> *It wasn't just that she was on bed rest; there were severe complications, too. We'd had a previous preemie, and I worried that we'd have another child with special needs.*
>
> ⌒ Kevin

Some men are intensely afraid for their partners and babies ("I was so afraid that she might die while I was away at work."). Others are much more hopeful than their partners are. For them, having to deal with their partner's anxiety is more stressful than dealing with their own.

Acknowledging and releasing feelings are always an important part of coping with a crisis. However, while we women typically derive support from many sources, men often rely on us, their partners, for their primary support. During bed rest, that support is, understandably, minimal.

Not wanting to cause further stress, your partner may also be reluctant to share his feelings. And, unless your health-care providers are very in tune to family needs during bed rest, your mate probably won't get the support he needs from those who are caring for you. At a time in his life when he really needs a listening ear, he may feel quite isolated.

> *I felt very unimportant, almost invisible. Everyone's attention was directed toward my wife and our baby. Of course, they should be the focus, but I was also scared, busy, and stressed. A few people did ask how I was, but most just asked about my wife.*
>
> ⌒ Matt

> *To most people, pregnancy complications mean morning sickness and swollen feet. No one really understood what it was like. Coworkers would make insensitive comments to me, like "Oh, your wife is in bed all day. Must be nice." Only five people offered to bring us meals during her fourteen weeks in bed.*
>
> ⌒ Kevin

For most couples, starting a conversation about feelings takes effort, but bear in mind that your relationship can grow and deepen if you share your feelings with each other. Try to encourage your partner to open up (use this chapter as a starting point). Talk about the uncertainties, the losses, and the adjustments that are all a part of a high-risk pregnancy.

When researching the effects of bed rest on fathers, Dr. Judith A. Maloni asked dads what helped them the most during their partners' confinement. They reported the greatest source of help was tangible assistance from family, friends, and neighbors. If you're reluctant to accept a helping hand for yourself, *do so for him.*

Men also need time-outs, says Deborah S. Simmons, a licensed family and marriage therapist, who survived three-and-a-half months of bed rest. "Just because you're sent to bed, doesn't mean he needs to be," she says. "The partner is often left out of support during bed rest, yet demands on him are constantly being made. This is a critical time for him to take care of himself; it's even an opportunity for him to make new friends."

> *Every couple of weeks I'd get someone to watch my daughter and I'd go play basketball. It gave me something to look forward to, and it took my mind off of things.*
>
> ⌒ Michael

For expectant fathers weathering the bed-rest storm, here are some suggestions from men who have been there:

- Focus more on the outcome of your efforts and less on the adverse impact of bed rest. Relatively speaking, this is a short time in your life, but those weeks and months of your partner's confinement can make a huge difference in your baby's life.

- Focus on getting through each day, and try not to think too much about tomorrow or the next day. Take it one day at a time. Remember, your wife won't be pregnant forever.

- Bed rest causes a change in your lifestyle, your routine, and your normal role in your relationship; this is bound to create some tension in the house. Quickly accept that this is not going to be easy, and talk openly and honestly about your feelings with your partner.

- Let yourself feel. Many men create tough exteriors during difficult times. It's okay to feel some anger, frustration, sadness, fear, guilt, and resentment. If feelings get in the way of your relationships, seek professional help.

- Don't suffer in silence. Reach out to others (a friend, a family member, a coworker, a clergy person, or a mental-health professional), and, again, don't be afraid to tell your mate how you're feeling. Another father who has been through the bed-rest experience can be a great source of advice and understanding. Referrals can be obtained from health-care professionals and volunteer groups (see Bed Rest/Support in appendix D).

- Lighten the load. Accept any and all offers of help. This isn't the time to be too proud to take a helping hand.

- Participate in the pregnancy and get to know your baby. Go to medical appointments, read pregnancy books, feel the baby kick, and talk to your baby.

- To keep your relationship strong, offer your partner patience, love, and reassurance. Stay in constant contact, and find innovative ways to help her pass the time.

- Ask for support from your partner, too. Don't be afraid to let her see you cry. She may appreciate the opportunity to think about someone other than herself and the baby for a while.

Some days, it may be difficult to support your mate when you're feeling very needy. Keep in mind that you are both going through a difficult time, and consider these ideas for offering support:

- Encourage your partner to take frequent short breaks. By using a pager, a cellular phone, or just by checking in regularly, he can stay available while taking time to rejuvenate. Suggest that he get some exercise, see a movie, or go to a sporting event with a friend.

- Acknowledge his efforts. Let him know that you appreciate everything he is doing for both you and the baby. Tell him you appreciate his physical support as well as his emotional support.

- Support your mate by doing small household jobs from bed, or plan a night out for him.

- Encourage your partner to sit quietly and do nothing once in a while. Men often need permission to *not* work.

- Create some fun. Bed rest is serious business and adding some laughter and fun can lessen the load. Watch a funny movie together, play a game, or send your mate a funny card.

- It bears repeating: Accept any and all offers of help, reducing your partner's workload.

IT TAKES TWO

Many women feel guilty when their partners have to carry more of the weight, so to speak, during their confinement. You must keep in mind that you did not cause your high-risk pregnancy and bed rest should be a team effort. His job is to take care of practical matters; your job is to grow your baby.

"While you may feel like your partner has the worst end of the deal, he or she may feel the same way about your end," says Dr. Stein.

> *I had it much easier than she did. I could leave the hospital and go to sleep at night. It was so hard for her to get any rest in the hospital.*
>
> ⟜ Michael

I had just known my husband for one year when I became completely dependent on him for nearly every one of my needs. Through the whole ordeal he just smiled and said "We'll get through this."

⌒ Sara

Rather than focus on what each of you is doing, focus on being a team. Also, give yourselves the opportunity to "not do and simply be," says Dr. Stein. While keeping life as normal as possible during a crisis helps, "acknowledging that life is anything but normal right now can be a tremendous relief," Dr. Stein adds. Take some time to breathe, reflect, and talk.

If your spouse isn't being a team player, you need to address why. Perhaps he really wasn't all that helpful before bed rest. If this is the case, this is not the time to try and change him, but you'll need to focus on resolving this potentially relationship-damaging issue once the baby arrives (some helpful books and resources are listed at the end of this chapter).

Perhaps your partner doesn't understand the risks involved if you don't comply with confinement, as is sometimes the case with first-time dads. Some men have a hard time understanding the need for bed rest because there isn't a visible illness, or they don't know how an early birth can affect the baby.

Your partner may even be in denial.

I kept thinking that maybe the doctors were wrong. I didn't want Barb to be on bed rest, so I didn't accept it. If I left the house feeling like she was okay, I could get through the day.

— Tim

A lack of support from your partner may make you feel resentful, confused, embarrassed, disappointed, and angry, as these mothers reveal:

My husband acted like bed rest was the worst thing that ever happened to him. I was the one whose life was changed dramatically and felt so guilty about it. For years, he claimed that he did all the household chores during that time (he didn't).

My husband insisted on playing golf two times a week for about five to six hours at a time. He should have been home taking care of our son and me so that others didn't have to. I hated making excuses for his behavior.

It can be helpful to do a little detective work to find out why your partner isn't helping more. He may need help acknowledging and soothing his anxieties (just as you do) before he can participate fully in the pregnancy. If your partner acts angry, it may be a cover for his sadness, fear, and helplessness. Ask your mate what he is angry about and don't assume that you are the cause.

Getting your partner more involved in the pregnancy may also help. Encourage him to attend medical appointments and learn about your condition and its risks. Seeing an ultrasound and listening to the baby's heartbeat can make the baby feel more real. Following the baby's development in a pregnancy book or on an interactive pregnancy Web site (see Who Can Help at the end of this chapter) can reinforce the need to postpone delivery for as long as possible.

> *The day I was put on bed rest my husband was annoyed at me. He thought my blood pressure was high because I had been eating too much salt and hadn't been swimming, as my doctor had instructed. When he came home that day to calm me down, he said he was going upstairs to change his clothes, but he was gone for a long time. When he came back down, he admitted that he was reading about preeclampsia. He apologized for thinking that I was somehow at fault.*
>
> ⤙ Barb

Receiving the support you need from your mate is critical, and you shouldn't be apologetic about your needs. "Ask for what you need in a confident manner, without being whiney or apologetic," says Laurie Krauth, a licensed psychotherapist and bed-rest veteran. "After all, this is your life partner and the baby belongs to both of you."

If you find yourself getting up to take care of yourself because your partner won't, then it's your responsibility to get outside assistance. If finances allow, hire help (your husband may notice the bills and start pitching in). Also, rely on your community (see Creating a Community Pregnancy in chapter 2).

"The bottom line is you can't do this alone," says Krauth. "You may need to be assertive, but you must take care of yourself and your baby."

An Opportunity for Closeness

Sexual relations, an important part of a loving relationship, are often limited or prohibited during a bed-rest pregnancy. If you're unsure of your sexual limitations, ask your doctor or a nurse for specific guidelines; some experts think that stimulation and arousal may cause early labor.

Certainly a lack of intimacy can cause some tension between couples, but it may not be as much a concern as you think. When Dr. Maloni researched the effects of bed rest on fathers, few identified the lack of sex as a problem. To most husbands, a successful pregnancy matters more than the desire for immediate gratification.

*We tried to remember that we had a lifetime of intimacy
ahead of us, and we only needed to refrain for a short time in
relation to our lives as a couple.*

⌒ Mark

Finding other ways to be affectionate—and talking about intimacy—may actually bring you closer.

*My husband and I had to be celibate for several months. It
turned out to be a turning point in our marriage. We
learned how to really talk to each other, and we developed a
closer intimacy than we had before.*

⌒ Allison

Talk about your feelings regarding your reduced sexual life, what
you both like, and what each of you does that feels good. Emphasize
what you can do together, such as cuddling and watching a movie.
Light some candles, play some soft music, and give each other a massage, or gently and lovingly stroke each other (if this is within your
doctor's guidelines).

*We tried to tell each other how important each was to the
other, and how much our lives have been enriched by being
together. Heartfelt expressions of love do wonders for relationships during bed rest.*

⌒ Erin

Holding hands while sleeping helped us feel connected!

                ⌒ Leslie

While in the hospital, my husband would tell me nice things about myself, like how strong I was and how much he loved me for being strong. One night he brought me some real food and we sat and listened to the fetal monitor. My favorite thing he did was rub my feet. It felt so good since I had them up in the air most of my stay and they got really numb.

                ⌒ Adrienne

I love my husband and felt bad that we couldn't be "active," but we held each other, cuddled, and used creative touch instead.

                ⌒ Jackie

Some couples send each other love letters or cards, or read out loud together. Others enjoy spreading a tablecloth on top of the bed and picnicking. Be creative. You'll reap an additional reward, too: Learning ways to foster closeness during bed rest will be quite helpful once the baby arrives—and there is less time and energy to focus on intimacy!

Who Can Help

Also see Who Can Help in chapter 9.

American Association for Marriage and Family Therapy
1133 15th St., N.W., Suite 300
Washington, DC 20005
(202) 452-0109
www.aamft.org

Collaborative Family Healthcare Coalition
P.O. Box 20838
Rochester, NY 14602
(716) 482-8210
www.cfhcc.org

For interactive pregnancy calendars:
www.babycenter.com
www.epregnancy.com
www.parentsplace.com

Recommended Reading

"Antepartum Bed Rest: Effect upon the Family" by Judith A.
Maloni, Jane E. Brezinski-Tomasi, and Laurie A. Johnson

(*Journal of Obstetric, Gynecologic and Neonatal Nursing*, 2001, Vol. 30, No. 2)

The Back Rub Book: How to Give and Receive Great Back Rubs by Anne Kent Rush (Vintage, 1989)

The Dance of Intimacy: A Woman's Guide to Courageous Acts of Change in Key Relationships by Harriet Lerner, Ph.D. (HarperCollins, 1990)

"Fathers' Experience of Their Partners' Antepartum Bed Rest" by Judith A. Maloni and M. Barbara Ponder (*Image: The Journal of Nursing Scholarship*, 1997, Vol. 29, No. 2)

Romantic Massage by Randy Nokola (Sterling Publications, 1997)

CHAPTER EIGHT

Siblings in Waiting

Parenting is not an easy job, even for those who are mobile. When mom is confined, the job becomes even more challenging. Mom's physical restrictions and dad's time limitations may influence the quality and amount of attention and care given to siblings.

> *I hated not being able to hold and carry my son. Even now,*
> *I feel like I cheated him out of so much when I was on bed*
> *rest.*
>
> — Jackie

Some parents say they feel as if they're sacrificing one child for another, an agonizing and heartbreaking position to be in. Sent to bed for preterm labor and gestational diabetes, Deborah S. Simmons, now a licensed marriage and family therapist, felt this parental tug-of-war. "One of my biggest concerns was how my bed rest might scar my daughter who was almost three," she says. "At the same time, I had an incredible need to care for my unborn baby."

Today, Dr. Simmons counsels many families coping with bed rest. She says that when parents and children join forces, most children, from tots to teens, not only survive their mom's bed rest—they thrive. But to make bed rest a family affair, you'll need to explain the importance of your confinement to your children, recognize when they need some tender loving care, and learn some special bedside parenting skills. This chapter addresses these three important areas.

WHAT'S WRONG WITH MOM?

For children, the world revolves around them, and you, the parents, are the axis. Your confinement makes your children's world tilt, perhaps even spin a little out of control. To get back on track, your children need to know how bed rest is going to affect their lives. They need age-appropriate explanations and honest answers to their questions.

First, Dr. Simmons suggests explaining that you need to lie down so the baby can stay inside of you and keep growing. Avoid using words like "sick" or "ill," which may make your child feel more anxious. If you're hospitalized, you can add that you and the baby need extra help from the doctors and nurses. Try not to overload your children with too much information. They'll ask questions when they need to know more.

I used two of my daughter's dolls, one tiny and one the size of a healthy newborn, to show her how big the baby in my tummy was and how big he needed to be before he could come out. Even at two-and-a-half, she grasped this concept.

⌒ Nina

Books with pictures of growing babies can demonstrate why it's best for the baby not to be born yet (see Recommended Reading for Siblings at the end of this chapter). Older children can benefit from a science lesson about the uterus and baby development. Explain that all mothers-to-be don't need bed rest, but some do. Also, because young children often believe in magical thinking (wishing so will make it come true), explain that your need to rest has nothing to do with anything your child or anyone else did.

Children often find their own ways of coping with bed rest: Some will ask thoughtful questions; some will play out events with dolls; others will pretend to be a nurse or doctor and take care of mommy. These are all healthy ways to make sense of an event that is unusual and confusing.

When the visiting nurse came, my daughter, who had just turned three, got out her doctor kit and helped the nurse examine me. When she was done, she'd announce, "Everything is just fine. I'll be back next week."

⌒ Leslie

Children of any age may harbor feelings of fear about their mother dying. "Even if they don't ask, you should address the death issue head on," advises Dr. Simmons. Explain that you only need to lie in bed or be in the hospital during pregnancy, and you'll be back to your old self once the baby arrives. If death is too difficult for you to discuss, have your partner, a close relative, or a friend talk to your child.

Young children may have a hard time understanding that bed rest is temporary. You can use a calendar or other visual aid to demonstrate how time passes and to explain the temporary nature of bed rest. Have your child check off each day and week of your pregnancy on a calendar. You can even celebrate each passing week with a special treat, such as borrowing a new video or book from the library or by learning a new card game.

For children who are old enough to understand the change in seasons, you can talk about special times that you shared in seasons past (for example, a nature walk when the leaves were changing colors) and tell them that you will be well enough to go on that walk again when that special season returns.

No matter what age, your children will want reassurance that you'll still be there for them. Explain to a young child that you can't play ball outside, but you can spend lots of time together by reading, coloring, and playing games on the bed. Assure older children that they'll still get to do most of their usual activities, and have regular talks about their daily activities, interests, friends, and school work.

STEPPING INTO YOUR CHILD'S SHOES

Our two-year-old really missed her mom. She basically didn't have anyone to play with for three months.

⸰— Michael

I thought my toddler would have more of a problem adapting to my bed rest, but she did great. I worried needlessly. After the first couple of weeks, she thought it was normal to have a mom in bed, and she even looked at me funny when I did get up.

⸰— Rachel

Bed rest causes major changes in a family's routine, so it's only natural for children to feel some resentment. Young children may not fully understand why mom can't care for them and play with them the way she did before bed rest. Children may not like caregivers taking mom's place, especially if sitters weren't frequently used before bed rest. If you're hospitalized, your children may miss you a great deal. Whining, sulking, demanding, regressing in development, and uncooperative behavior are all typical responses.

Older children may resent having to take over household tasks or missing activities. Jealousy may arise when parents, preoccupied with mom's needs and the expectant baby's needs, have little leftover energy and time for them. Older children miss their moms (and dads), too. They may become angry, uncooperative, and uncommunicative.

Temporary behavior problems and emotional distress in children during their mom's bed rest are common. Encouraging your children to express their feelings by drawing pictures of the baby, writing letters to the baby, or playing with puppets or dolls can help. Offering your children time and a listening ear are essential. "Just as you need your worries heard and validated, so do your children," says psychologist Mara Stein. "During bed rest, they need honest information and reassurance that you're okay and that you love them more than ever."

> *When Megan woke up from her naps, I'd have my helpers bring her to me and we'd cuddle and talk for a bit.*
>
> ⌒ Rachel

If your child displays warning signs, such as continued developmental regression, withdrawing, sleep disturbances, unusual complaining about stomachaches or other illnesses, destructive behavior, or perfect behavior (doing everything right to please you), consult your pediatrician or another child development expert, such as a trained therapist.

PRACTICAL TIPS FOR PILLOW PARENTING

When I was in the hospital, my husband would visit me every day during his lunch hour. At night, he would go home and eat dinner with our two-year-old and put her to bed, trying to make life for her as normal as possible.

— Leah

"The more normal you can keep life during bed rest, the easier life will be for your children," says Dr. Simmons. This means trying to stick to regular schedules, including meals, bedtimes, and activities.

Once again, you'll need help from friends, family, neighbors, and volunteers, and you may need to hire a caregiver or trade services for baby-sitting. Telephone calls, keeping a calendar, and managing helpers will become an important part of your day (unless it becomes too stressful, then you need to delegate). Remember to give caregivers clear instructions and support their efforts.

You should also try to keep the same family rules and household responsibilities that you had before bed rest (even though leniency may be tempting, and children may sometimes try to take advantage of mom's downtime).

When the going gets tough, remember: Consistency is the key to helping your children feel more secure. "Your children need to see that you are the same competent mom that you were before bed rest," says Dr. Stein. "Pushing limits can be a way to test how resilient and competent you really are. Seeing you stay relatively calm and consistent can be very reassuring to a child."

Family rituals, such as birthday parties and holiday celebrations, should also continue. However, flexibility and creativity are now needed. If you're the one who usually hosts holidays, you can still do so by having others prepare meals or by ordering takeout. If you usually bake a cake, consider buying or bartering for one this year. "Keep your ritual, but add something new and different," suggests Dr. Simmons. "And try not to place additional burden on your partner's shoulders."

I missed my daughter's trip to see Santa. My parents took her instead. They called me from a cellular phone and told me, play by play, about the day.

— Rachel

The following are some more ideas from veteran bed-rest moms and family-care experts for making bedside parenting a little easier. Keep in mind that some suggestions may not be appropriate for your medical condition.

- Every day, schedule some time to be alone with your child. With so many helpers, it's sometimes hard to get important one-on-one time. Read, sing, cuddle, and talk together.

- Have caregivers do some daily activities near your bed-rest post, allowing you to participate verbally and encourage your child's development.

- Keep a special basket or tub of toys, games, books, and easy art projects by your bedside (at home or in the hospital). An old sheet, blanket, or a cafeteria tray can keep the couch or comforter clean.

- Some moms and children like having a weekly schedule to look forward to: Mondays are for play dates (at your home or a friend's); Tuesdays and Fridays are for Grandma's house or day-care center; Wednesdays and Thursdays are for helpers at home.

- To reduce stress and worry, try to plan ahead for special events, appointments, and lessons. Make a family calendar, and inform your partner and primary helpers about important dates. Line up drivers and helpers (maybe even a backup helper) in advance. Confirm arrangements a day or two before the event.

- When helpers watch your children, exchange contact phone numbers and provide them with any necessary items, such as spending money, extra clothes, or sunscreen.

- Assign a helper "gift duty." Stock up on birthday and other gifts. You can also shop on the Internet or through catalogs. You may even save money by buying bulk.

- Keep an updated list of names and phone numbers for emergency child care.

- For important occasions, have your partner, a family member, or a friend take your place and videotape. Borrow a camcorder, if you don't have one. Watch the tape with your child. Instant-photograph cameras are also a good way for you to record and share events. You may also consider asking your doctor if using a wheelchair to attend the event is possible. You can rent one from a local home health-care supply company.

- Make school-break arrangements well in advance. Many camps fill up fast.

- Tell the teachers and other appropriate school personnel about your family's situation. They can be on the lookout for behavioral and developmental warning signs, as well as provide some extra attention your child might need.

MAKING BED REST A FAMILY AFFAIR

My children, ten and six, were my best supporters. They played games with me and brought me water. I was so proud of them!

— Kendra

Giving your children the opportunity to help during bed rest will make them feel more in control. Working together as a team can also strengthen your family bond. Children learn responsibility and independence (good preparation for baby's arrival), and you benefit from an extra set of helping hands—even if they are small!

Children as young as three can participate in pregnancy by talking to the baby, rubbing your tummy, and helping you pass the time. A young child can bring items to you, deliver messages to family members, and help with meal preparation.

Older children can handle age-appropriate tasks, such as vacuuming, picking up, taking out the garbage, and yard work. Avoid assigning big jobs that may require supervision, such as cleaning out the garage. Children can also go through the pantry and refrigerator and make a grocery list.

At the start of each week, have a family meeting and discuss each person's contribution and the week's agenda. (This is a good time to address concerns and feelings, too.) Don't apologize for needing help, but do acknowledge your children's important roles. By recognizing that bed rest is a challenge your entire family faces, your children will take pride in helping to bring their sibling to life.

The following ideas can help your family unite during bed rest and also have some fun. Again, keep in mind that some may not be appropriate for your medical condition.

- Every day, share at least one meal together as a family, even if it's on top of the bed. Mealtimes are great conversation starters.

- Make assembly lines for getting jobs, like dishwashing and laundry, done.

- Host a weekly bedside movie-and-pizza party.

- Pretend your bed is an "island" surrounded by water. Your child can "fish" off the side using magnets, cutout fish, and paperclips. Your child can jump into the "water" and take a "swim." Talk about what the "island" looks like and who will rescue you.

- Tell progressive stories: One says a sentence and others take turns adding on sentences.

- "Camp out" together. Tell ghost stories under the sheets. Make shadow figures on the walls and eat popcorn.

- Create new family rituals. During her bed rest, Dr. Simmons and her family began turning out the lights at bedtime and chatting. Today, her eight- and eleven-year-old still enjoy these end-of-the-day chats.

A BED-REST BONUS

Many families who have survived bed rest say the crisis actually created some positive changes. For instance, fathers often form strong bonds with their children during mom's confinement, a closeness that continues long after the new baby's arrival.

Sure I felt sad that I missed a few months of my daughter's childhood, but she built a great bond with her father.

⸺ Rachel

Jealousy that often follows the birth of a new brother or sister may be less because children aren't as dependent on mom and dad. They now know others can take care of them, too.

I was a little worried how my son would react when the baby, who had already disrupted our lives so much, was born. He wasn't affected at all. We took him to the hospital, and he just kept touching the baby and saying "Look how soft," and "So cute."

⸺ Jackie

Newly discovered independence, and pride for helping to "grow" the baby, can also make sibling adjustment easier.

I continue to be amazed at the grace in which my daughter, ,at age three, expanded her concept of family and accepted her brother into her world. I think my being on bed rest helped because we talked about the baby every day, and I explained how her cooperation was helping to make him strong and

*healthy. She has a strong feeling today that she "owns" the
baby because she had a role in bringing him into the world.*

⌒ Nina

After you reach the end of the bed-rest tunnel, chances are you,
too, will not only be rewarded with a healthy baby, but with a closer-
knit family as well.

WHO CAN HELP

See Who Can Help in chapters 7 and 9.

RECOMMENDED READING FOR SIBLINGS

And Mommy's on Her Side: A Children's Book About Bedrest by Heidi
Travis (A Place to Remember, 2000)

Are You My Mother? by P. D. Eastman (Random House, 1998)

Before You Were Born by Jennifer Davis (Workman, 1998)

Carrying by Gwenyth Swain (Carolrhoda Books, 1999)

*Dr. Amelia's Boredom Survival Guide: First Aid for Rainy Days,
Boring Errands, Waiting Rooms, Whatever!* by Marissa Moss
(Pleasant Company Publications, 1999)

"Helpful Hints for Bedrest: Entertaining Children," a handout (Sidelines National Support Network, 1997)

Let's Talk About Having a New Brother or Sister by Diana Star Helmer (Powerkids Press, 1999)

"Mommy and the Hospital," a coloring book, by Beth Mosele and Aileen Mosele (send a self-addressed 8½ × 11 envelope with three stamps to: Beth Mosele, The Methodist Hospital, Care Management Dept., Mail Code D1246565 Fannin, Houston, TX 77030)

Mommy's in the Hospital Having a Baby by Maxine B. Rosenberg (Clarion, 1997)

"My Mommy Is on Bedrest," a coloring book (A Place to Remember, 2000)

What to Expect When Mommy's Having a Baby by Heidi Murkoff (HarperFestival, 2000)

Fun Web sites:
www.bonus.com
www.cartoonnetwork.com
disney.com
www.exploratorium.com
www.familyfun.com

www.gustown.com

www.howstuffworks.com

www.kidlink.org

kids.discover.com

pbskids.org

CHAPTER NINE

Coming to Terms with Confinement

We must be willing to get rid of the life we've planned, so as to have the life that is waiting for us.

⌐ Joseph Campbell

When you first discovered that your pregnancy was complicated, you may have felt a whirlwind of emotions: confusion, shock, fear, anger, disappointment, resentment, guilt, and sadness. A bed-rest prescription added to your emotional turmoil. After all, you've now been sentenced to bed and your before-baby bliss has been destroyed. A bed-rest pregnancy causes many losses; to come to terms with this, you must let yourself feel and grieve.

Many women on bed rest find it comforting to learn that their feelings are normal, that others in a similar situation feel the same way they do. This chapter shares some of the common reactions to a bed-rest prescription. You may find yourself saying, "That's how I feel!" Ways to lessen the anxiety and stress that often accompany these feelings are addressed in the second half of the chapter.

How You May Be Feeling

From my own experience, when I was first told to put my feet up, I actually felt relieved. I'd been spotting on and off for several weeks and following bed-rest orders was at least something I could do to help my baby. Psychologist Mara Stein, who was teaching graduate courses, supervising a student, seeing patients—and carrying twins!—was also relieved to head to bed. "I was dying for someone to tell me to slow down," she says. "I just didn't expect to have to slow down that much!"

At first, many moms, like Dr. Stein and me, think bed rest will be similar to taking a vacation, providing time to rest, relax, and rejuvenate. But as you probably learned quickly, bed rest is anything but restful. Throughout this book, the many challenges of a bed-rest prescription have been addressed, from setting up your room, to eating properly, to maintaining relationships, to parenting. Now it's time to talk about *you*: how you're feeling about your pregnancy and how you're coping with the changes in your life. Let's begin.

"I've Lost All Control!"

Before bed rest, you were probably an active woman with a busy schedule. You may have been working outside of the home, or you were a stay-at-home mom. Perhaps you participated in a regular exercise program, did volunteer work, or had a full social calendar. You didn't expect your pregnancy to significantly impact these activities, but it did.

Depending on your doctor's directions, you may have had to stop working or caring for your children full time. Walking to the kitchen to fix a meal, answering the door, and driving to the store may now be out of the question. Many women compare at-home bed rest to being a prisoner under house arrest.

If you're hospitalized, you must rely extensively on the nurses. You may even need permission to stand and use the bathroom. At times, you probably feel like a child, with your medical team taking on a parenting role.

> *I hated not being able to help myself and having to depend on others. I really missed my job, where I was in total control.*
>
> ⟶ Teri

You may also feel as though your body is controlling you, rather than you controlling your body. This is often the case when bed rest is doing little to relieve symptoms. Leah describes her early feelings this way: "My life and head were spinning. I couldn't make any decisions. Nothing got done. I had lost all control of my body and my head."

Feeling powerless and helpless are common throughout bed rest, but particularly so during those early days and weeks when you're adjusting to a drastically changed lifestyle. Relinquishing control and allowing others to care for you will take time.

> *Bed rest is an emotional roller-coaster ride. It is definitely very hard work. But it can be a chance to grow as a human, a couple, and a family. I learned how to ask for help clearly and how to give clear directions. I learned how to let go of what was outside of my control.*
>
> ⤝ Erin

For some women, finding ways to regain a sense of control can help. Sticking to a regular routine can give you control of your day. (If you're hospitalized, inform your medical team about your desire for a daily schedule.) Also, assist with easy-to-do household chores, and manage your bed rest by keeping a family calendar, making phone calls, and planning meals. Learning about your pregnancy and condition and keeping your medical team well informed of any changes or concerns will also provide you with some feelings of control.

> *I kept a journal of my blood pressure, symptoms, and my peak flows (I have asthma). This made me feel like I was at*

least doing something productive to help myself; it gave me
some control.

⌒ Barb

For other women, just letting time pass and getting through the day is enough (and it *is* a big accomplishment). You shouldn't feel compelled to take charge of your life during bed rest if that doesn't appeal to you, says Dr. Stein. "For some women, bed rest is the beginning of a journey of change. You don't feel like yourself, and so you're not motivated to do the things that you used to do. Accept this if it is how you feel. It won't last forever."

In short, do what *you* need to do to get through your days in waiting.

"Who Am I?"

Along with a loss of control, you may also experience a loss of self because you can't do the things you normally would: unfinished work may be left to coworkers; others must care for your children; and household roles are reversed, with your partner taking over your usual duties.

I hated the person I had become. I am normally a go-getter
and pride myself on meeting deadlines, having a clean

house, and getting things done. Even though I felt just fine, I had to lie there and watch others do for me. I probably shouldn't have, but I worried a lot about what others thought of me: Did they think I was just lazy?

⌒ Allison

Most days I felt like I didn't have anything to talk about because I hadn't done anything. I just wanted my old self back!

⌒ Lisa

Being treated as if you're ill (when you may feel perfectly fine) doesn't help either. Some women who have been on bed rest say their loved ones and health-care providers treated them as if they were victims: Rather than talking to them directly about their pregnancy, they talked among themselves in hushed voices. While only trying to protect you, such actions can leave you feeling helpless and vulnerable. As one woman says, "There I was, lying in the hospital, tilted back, not able to move an inch. I felt like a completely incompetent person and that others were treating me this way."

Furthermore, bed rest can also change your perceptions of yourself. "When pregnancy doesn't go as expected, when you cannot control your life, you may begin to rethink your attitudes and goals," says Dr. Stein. "You may wonder what you are meant to learn from this experience and where you should go from here. You are likely to come out of this experience a very different person from who you were when you began bed rest."

Though it's normal to think about how bed rest has affected your many roles—as a woman, a mother, a wife, a daughter, and an employee—you now have a new, important job: growing your baby. Take pride in what you're doing, and don't let others deny you a sense of self-worth.

> *A woman who complies with bed rest has such courage: She makes drastic changes for the sake of her child! I would encourage any woman on bed rest to realize that they are their own higher power. The strength needed to get through bed rest and to do it as thoroughly as possible is within ourselves; it is there because we love our children.*
>
> — Kendra

"Why Is This Happening?"

Your life has completely changed without much, if any, warning. Who wouldn't be a little angry? Certain events and people may trigger your anger. For example, you may become angry if someone disappoints you, if information is not available, or if a member of your health-care team is evasive. In these cases, you have the right to feel angry and to seek the help, information, and support you need.

I was angry with my doctor and his staff for putting me on bed rest with no suggestions about how to deal with it. There are side effects that follow a bed-rest prescription, but no one seemed to care about them. I realize doctors aren't counselors, but just asking if I was okay would have been nice.

⌒ Lisa

You may also find yourself angry with your own body ("I was very upset with my body for betraying me!"), or angry at a wide range of sources.

I was angry with the doctors, the medical field, my body, God, and the whole world! I had wanted kids for as long as I can remember. Through the years, I'd heard so many stories of women who took horrid care of their bodies yet still had normal pregnancies. Why couldn't life be easy for me just once?

⌒ Erin

You may become uncharacteristically irritable and easily upset at even the smallest surprises, such as a cancelled TV show or a delayed visit. When this happens, try to identify the real source of your anger. Are you angry because you're bored and were looking forward to watching television or talking with a friend? Then seek some other ways to reduce that boredom. Is it the lack of control over your life that's making you mad? Finding some ways to feel more in control may help.

Avoid releasing your anger toward others (particularly those who are helping you) by finding some constructive ways to "let it all out." Make a list of the things that make you mad, or write a letter to the person you are angry with (but don't send it). If your doctor allows, exercise using the suggestions in chapter 6. Yell, if it helps. One woman borrowed her son's toy gun and shot foam bullets at a target. Don't keep your anger inside: Releasing feelings is an important part of working through your pain.

"Why Can't I Have a Normal Pregnancy?"

Toward the end of my first bed rest, a friend hosted a baby shower for two other expectant moms and me. I "cheated" (though I don't advise this) and went to her home, spending most of the time in a recliner. The two other moms-to-be chatted about shopping for their babies, decorating nurseries, and attending childbirth classes. All things I couldn't do, of course. Once again, I felt like a complete failure, a feeling that kept surfacing ever since I'd been labeled a high-risk mom.

Guilt is one of the hardest emotions to overcome during bed rest, especially since there is so much time for self-reflection. We blame ourselves for not having a normal pregnancy, for our family's emo-

tional and financial stresses, for cheating and attending baby show-
ers, or for not being happier when the pregnancy test came back positive.

> *I wondered what I had done to cause this terrible thing to*
> *occur. I felt tremendous guilt because I was unhappy when I*
> *first learned I was pregnant.*
>
> — Caroline

> *I was embarrassed that I wasn't "normal." No one in my*
> *huge family had experienced any problems during preg-*
> *nancy, and I got the feeling that some people just thought I*
> *was being dramatic.*
>
> *I also felt as though I was letting my husband down by*
> *not being able to bear children in a normal fashion. I mean,*
> *women have been having babies for millions of years, right?*
> *How hard could it be?*
>
> — Barb

Guilt and self-blame require energy that could be better directed
toward managing your bed rest and growing your baby. Learning
about your pregnancy and talking with others who have experienced
a similar problem can help you understand that you're not at fault.
Ask your medical team as many questions as needed. There is no

such thing as a stupid question: Ask about anything you think may have caused your complications. Putting your fears to rest will free you to focus on your pregnancy.

You can also refer to the books listed at the end of chapter 1 and the resources listed under Complications in Pregnancy in appendix D. Most importantly, try not to spend your days in waiting thinking about what you did wrong or what might have been—focus on what you're doing right.

> *I have found with my own bed-rest experiences that once things are moving along as smoothly as possible, it can be a very peaceful time. Serenity after the shock of bed rest will come if you let go of your guilt. The depressing days will come, too (we are, after all, only human), but peace and serenity can return if you let it.*
>
> ⌒ Kendra

"Will My Baby Be Okay?"

"Being put on bed rest is like entering a new world, where you don't know anything, and you're trying desperately to catch up," says Dr. Stein. "It can be terrifying, especially if your pregnancy has gone awry long before your baby can be safely delivered."

Fear, uncertainty, instability, worry, and anxiety go hand in hand with a high-risk pregnancy. As much as you try to focus on the positive, there is always that underlying question: Will my baby be okay?

> *Starting bed rest at ten weeks makes for a very long and worrisome pregnancy. Just once I wanted to have confidence in a pregnancy, instead of fear.*
>
> ∽ Kendra

> *I was often afraid. I was terrified and nervous about the possibility of losing the baby. I was apprehensive and even a bit insecure. Pregnancy is hard on your hormones anyway, and bed rest certainly added to my moods!*
>
> ∽ Teri

> *I was terrified of having another preemie. I knew just enough to really scare me.*
>
> ∽ Erin

> *Bed rest is a bad thing when you are worried because there is little else to distract you.*
>
> ∽ Leah

When I was pregnant with my second son, I postponed buying baby items, thinking about a name, and talking to him until I passed twenty-eight weeks (when my first son was born). If I didn't get too attached to this little person inside of me, it wouldn't hurt so much should the worst happen. Not wanting to cause my husband, family, and friends more worry, I also kept my fears inside; this only made me feel worse.

"Distancing yourself from your baby does not protect you; in fact, it can rob you of valuable time with your little one," says Dr. Stein. Acknowledging and talking about your fears—that your baby may die or be born far too soon—is an important part of healing. Coming to terms with your fears will more fully allow you to participate in your pregnancy, too.

If you're uncomfortable sharing thoughts with loved ones, reach out to someone else (a nurse, a home health-care aide, a social worker, a clergy person, or a mental-health expert). Write your thoughts down in a notebook. Seek bed-rest veterans through the Internet or referrals from your health-care team.

"The Days Are So Long!"

Some days Teri looked at her clock every twenty minutes and time seemed to drag. "Those days I just wanted to hop into my car and drive far away from everything and everyone. Other days were much easier," she says.

On bed rest, time may seem like your enemy, but it isn't. The passing of each hour, day, week, or month is a precious gift to your baby.

When boredom becomes unbearable, remind yourself that every day your baby stays within your womb is one more day closer to a healthy delivery.

Chapter 3 provides ideas for escaping the tediousness of bed rest. Moving your bed-rest nest to a different location within your home, or even a different house, can also help.

Also, ask your doctor if you can leave the house by reclining in the backseat of a car or by taking a wheelchair. One woman went to the movies once a week by having a friend drop her off and pick her up at the theater's door.

If you're hospitalized, ask the nurses what options are available for long-term patients. If your condition has stabilized, your doctor may allow a once-a-day wheelchair ride around the hall, or around the hospital to the gift shop or the cafeteria. Perhaps you can sit outside in the sun for a while (you'll need a friend or hospital volunteer to go with you). If things go well, you may even get a "temporary pass" for a few hours to go out to dinner. One hospitalized mother was "released" to visit her children at home.

"No One Understands!"

Bed rest in the hospital or at home creates times of solitary confinement, when you feel completely alone and out of touch. Even when surrounded by people, you can feel lonely; unless they've experienced a high-risk pregnancy and bed rest, friends, family members, and helpers may not understand the emotional and physical difficulties you're going through.

> *Some people didn't take my bed-rest sentence seriously, and it was hard to explain all the things that could happen if I didn't adhere to the doctor's orders. Since I felt pretty good physically, even my husband would sometimes lose sight of why I was banished to the couch, and that was really difficult. Many people who have never been pregnant or had an easy, normal pregnancy aren't aware of the complications and consequences of high-risk pregnancies. Having to explain all that "stuff" definitely didn't help.*
>
> — Barb

The importance of finding someone to talk to about your feelings has been mentioned throughout this book. There are people who will understand and support you, but you must be willing to reach out to them. With a Little Help from a Friend on page 165 suggests ways to find supportive people.

"Some Days I Just Want to Cry!"

You will experience good days and bad days, good moments and bad moments, during your bed rest. Mood swings are common throughout any pregnancy and dealing with medical issues and bed rest can compound them. One minute you may be laughing at a funny TV show, when suddenly a baby commercial makes you start crying. At times, you may feel sorry for yourself; other times, you're on top of the world.

Certain events, dates, or people can be particularly upsetting. Hospitalized women often become tearful when their families leave in the evenings, just as at-home moms may become upset when their spouses drive off for work. An anniversary date of a difficult milestone or stage during a previous pregnancy can trigger tears. Visits from certain people can be tough. Try to identify and address causes of your sadness, but also know that it's okay to feel sad for no apparent reason.

> *I accepted every mood I felt at that moment without analyzing why I felt that way. Being confined to bed is such an extreme situation that it is only normal, in my mind, to feel the extremes of all emotions. Accepting that you will feel uncomfortable emotions and expecting them is half the battle of eventually conquering them and achieving peace.*
>
> ⌒ Kendra

Fatigue can also play a part in your moods. Many women say they feel more tired during bed rest than before bed rest. Lying in bed all day, taking daytime naps, and around-the-clock hospital checks can interrupt your nighttime rest. If you're resting in bed during the day, consider changing to another room, or try to spend some time outdoors (if the weather and your doctor permit). Reduce the frequency or length of naps and find ways to keep busy. If you're hospitalized, ask the staff if nighttime procedures can be postponed until morning. Consult your doctor if your fatigue continues.

Though mood swings are normal, it's important to recognize the signs of depression. If you find that you are feeling sad most of the time, or you're beginning to withdraw from family, friends, and helpers, you may need professional help. Ask your doctor, a hospital caregiver, or local mental-health association for a referral. Some therapists will provide counseling over the telephone.

There is also much you can do to help yourself through your days in waiting, as the rest of this chapter discusses.

Taking Care of Yourself

Finding a way to reduce stress during your bed rest is important to your health and your baby's health. This may mean having a friend give you a daily massage, spending an hour listening to comforting music, or writing down your thoughts in a journal. You'll need to choose the method that best suits your personality and needs. The next sections offer some self-care suggestions.

With a Little Help from a Friend

Though it may appear that you're the center of attention with others waiting on you hand and foot, you may in fact be receiving very little emotional support. It's hard to ask those who are giving so much already also to listen to your problems and concerns. But along with practical care, you need emotional care, too.

Most women who successfully sustain bed rest say they couldn't have survived without the support of a bed-rest buddy; someone who truly understands what a complicated pregnancy and confinement is like. Through visits, the telephone, or the Internet, a bed-rest buddy can listen with the heart and respond with experience.

My best friend was pregnant at the same time I was and was also having complications. We were on bed rest at the same time, and it was great to whine to someone who knew exactly what I was going through.

— Erin

I don't know how I would have made it through bed rest without Carole, a woman whose face I never saw until five months after my bed rest ended. We met on the computer (she'd had twins, too) and stayed connected through a lap-

top when I was hospitalized. I don't know how she managed it, but she was always there when I logged on.

∽ Gwen

Many women on bed rest complain that none of their friends visit; but, I felt so nasty all the time, since I couldn't shower, it was almost a relief not to have visitors. I made a chat room on the Web so I could have my cyber-friends "over" every day.

∽ Rachel

To find a support person or group, ask your doctor or hospital staff for a referral. Your hospital may have weekly gatherings of bed-resting women. Don't be shy about joining in: These women are all in the same boat you are. If you can't leave your room, ask if you can talk to other hospitalized pregnant women over the phone. Friends and family may connect with other families of women on bed rest, too.

The national high-risk pregnancy and bed-rest support group, Sidelines, is listed in appendix D under Bed Rest/Support. At the time of this writing, Sidelines just finished their eighth year of providing support to over 35,000 expectant moms, and they have over 5,200 volunteers throughout the world.

Most of the major parenting Web sites host bed-rest E-mail lists and message boards (see appendix D). You can also join the Bed Rest Book Buddies through www.pregnancybedrest.com.

The Mighty Pen

Writing in a journal is an excellent way to relieve stress. A journal is never too tired to listen, it doesn't judge you, its feelings never get hurt, and it's free. You can write about your anger or sadness, then close the book and put away those feelings. If friends and family aren't supportive, it can be comforting to imagine showing your words to them some day. Your journal can also be a chronicle of your journey toward becoming a new mother. You can even make lists of things you are grateful for, as a reminder that life really isn't so bad.

Remember, though, that honest writing may stir up some intense feelings. You may feel relief from writing, but you may also feel an urge to talk to someone afterward.

Some books to help you start journaling are listed at the end of this chapter.

Take a Deep Breath

If you've never tried to relieve stress through a relaxation method, such as deep breathing or meditation, now is a good time to give it a try. Some instructional books and tapes are listed at the end of this chapter. Many childbirth instruction tapes also teach relaxation and breathing techniques. Try a few methods to find the one that works best for you.

The Power of Positive Thinking

I spent several hours each day talking to my baby, massaging my belly, and practicing conscious relaxation and positive visualization.

— Caroline

Positive thoughts often bring positive results. Try to spend some time each day (fifteen to twenty minutes is a good start) focusing on some of the good things bed rest has created: friendships with the people who are helping you; the increased quality time you're enjoying with family members; catching up on all those books you've

---

Bed Rest's Silver Lining

The Top-Ten Benefits of Taking Pregnancy Lying Down

by Laurie Krauth*

1. My husband has learned to cook (and not just in the microwave!), and he can now run the house. He no longer puts the first load of wash in the machine and leaves it until it's moldy. He regularly fills—and empties!—the dishwasher, notices when we're out of milk, creates a shopping list, buys in bulk, and looks for sales.

2. I am amassing a quantity of sleep that I won't see again until my baby is two.

3. I am enjoying gossiping with friends with a laziness that my baby won't permit again until preschool.

4. I'm losing my type-A personality. Before this bed-rest thing, I couldn't talk on the phone or have a friend over without also cooking or filing papers.

5. My old definition of a top-flight evening (one spent knocking off eight items on my to-do list) has been replaced by one spent watching two videos with my husband.

6. I can stare aimlessly into space (without mentally adding tasks to my to-do list).

7. My athletic virtuosity no longer depends upon one sweaty set of tennis, three jogs, and a night of swing dancing each week. Tackling the stairs now makes me proud.

8. I relish my baby's increasingly zealous kickboxing because I know he's well and happy—and that matters more than anything.

9. All this lying around has finally put a stop to my obsessive worries about handling the transition to motherhood, leaving in its wake the searing desire to get on with toughening up my nipples and changing diapers for my little kickboxer. I am ready to have this baby!

10. I'm actually looking forward to being liberated by childbirth. While my fellow expectant mothers anticipate losing mobility and independence, I can't wait to end bed rest and carry my baby out into the world. I'll be free!

*Laurie wrote this top-ten list while spending her last month of pregnancy in bed.

always wanted to read; or the time for self-reflection. Visualize what your family will do together once the baby arrives. Replace negative thoughts and words with more positive ones, read inspirational books, such as the *Chicken Soup for the Soul* series, and imagine delivering a healthy, full-term baby.

Most importantly, try to be your own cheerleader. Like the little engine in the children's classic, *The Little Engine That Could*, often tell yourself "I think I can. I think I can. I think I can." Positive attitudes are contagious, and you may soon find others cheering you on.

WHO CAN HELP

Also see Who Can Help in chapter 7.

American Psychiatric Association
1400 K St., N.W.
Washington, DC 20005
(888) 357-7924
www.psych.org

American Psychological Association
750 First St., N.E.
Washington, DC 20002
(800) 374-2721
www.apa.org

RECOMMENDED READING

Creative Visualization Workbook by Shakti Gawain (New World Library, 1995)

Dr. Susan Lark's Anxiety and Stress Self Help Book by Susan M. Lark, M.D. (Celestial Arts, 1996)

Expecting Change: The Emotional Journey Through Pregnancy by Ellen Sue Stern (Simon & Schuster, 1986) (out of print; check your library or used bookstore)

The New Diary by Tristine Rainer (Tarcher/Putnam, 1979)

One to One: Self-Understanding Through Journal Writing by Christina Baldwin (M. Evans & Co., 1992)

The Power of Positive Thinking by Norman Vincent Peale (Ballantine, 1996)

The Relaxation Response by Herbert Benson, M.D., and Miriam Z. Klipper (Wholecare, 2000)

SUGGESTED LISTENING

Creating the World You Really Want by Wayne W. Dyer and Deepak Chopra, M.D. (Hay House, 1998)

Meditation for Beginners by Jack Kornfield (Sounds True, 1998)

A Mother's Lullaby Audiocassette: Relaxation, Meditation, Bonding for Pregnancy (Heartpaths, 2000)

Relax & Enjoy Your Baby: A Complete Program of Relaxation for New & Expectant Parents by Sylvia Klein Olkin (Relaxation Co., 1996)

Why Me, Why This, Why Now: A Guide to Answering Life's Toughest Questions by Robin Norwood (Audio Renaissance, 1994)

CHAPTER TEN

Back on Your Feet!

Challenges are what make life interesting: Overcoming them is what makes life meaningful.

⟜ Joshua H. Marine

After eighteen weeks of modified and complete bed rest, Erin delivered a healthy baby boy. Relieved to put her second bed-rest experience behind her, Erin eagerly resumed the life she'd put on hold for so long. But getting back into the swing of things, including caring for three children under age four, wasn't so easy. "My back ached and I had nerve problems with my feet and ankles," says Erin. "It took nearly six months before I could lift and hold my children. I just couldn't get my strength back."

There was an emotional price to pay for her weeks of immobility, too: Returning to daily living was overwhelming, says Erin. "On bed rest I had a routine and space to myself. When it was over, everyone was suddenly making demands of me, and I had very little energy. I felt like I had to make up for missed time, but I couldn't."

Friends and family may think you should be rejuvenated after weeks of "rest," but you may actually be feeling sluggish and weak, even sad. Most bed-rest veterans say returning to the world after confinement was as difficult as the bed-rest term itself, perhaps even more so because friends, family, and health-care professionals didn't understand their post-bed-rest difficulties.

> *All of a sudden I was thrown back into a world of move-*
> *ment, and everyone seemed to have forgotten that I was just*
> *completely immobile for weeks.*
>
> ⌒ Sara

> *My doctor never even addressed what it would be like to*
> *return to normal living after so many weeks of staying off*
> *my feet. I was completely shocked to discover how painful it*
> *was to stand. I had this beautiful baby to care for, but hardly*
> *any strength to hold him. I was ashamed to tell anyone, but,*
> *for several weeks after his birth, all I wanted to do was crawl*
> *back into bed and sleep.*
>
> ⌒ Allison

> *My husband expected me to get up and get on with my life so*
> *he could stop doing everything. I did my best, but after four-*

teen weeks on bed rest and a C-section, I would just collapse at some point during the day. This caused a lot of friction between us.

⌒ Leslie

If you experienced complications during delivery, your baby was born early, or your baby died, recovery after bed rest becomes even more complicated. You need to recover from your bed-rest pregnancy, yet your energy, time, and attention are focused elsewhere. To help you cope with your feelings, giving you more strength for self-care, some helpful support groups and resources are listed in appendix D under Bereavement, Complications in Pregnancy, and Premature Birth.

This chapter will affirm that your aches and pains—both those in your body as well as those in your mind—are normal side effects of weeks or months of inactivity. If you're reading this before your baby's delivery, these pages will prepare you for what's ahead, reducing potential stress. "Women who are aware of bed rest's side effects and options for managing them may recover with less frustration," says Dr. Judith A. Maloni, who is one of only a few researchers who have studied the aftermath of bed rest.

If you're reading this after your baby's arrival, the following sections will help you make a smoother transition to vertical living.

TAKING A STAND

Depending on your situation, your bed-rest ban may be reduced or lifted before your baby's arrival. Weeks or months of little or no standing and walking and the weight of your baby may throw you off balance and cause some discomfort. Walking to stimulate labor may cause excessive strain on your muscles. You may need to remind the nurses about your bed-rest history, as well as to inform them about the muscle weakness that often occurs. Fatigue may also make it difficult for you to push during the second stage of labor.

If you're getting back on your feet after baby's birth, how quickly you recover will depend on the length and limitations of your bed rest. The longer your bed-rest sentence and the more severely your activity was restricted, the longer your recovery will take. A Caesarean section, delivery problems, or ongoing medical concerns can increase recovery time.

After six weeks of bed rest in the Trendelenburg position (head lower than legs), it hurt to lie horizontal! My muscles ached up and down my back, and it felt weird to lie flat instead of tilted back.

— Danielle

During labor I found that I had to make a distinct change in my mindset: I needed to encourage contractions, rather than

stop them. Pushing wasn't a big issue, though. One push and
he was out!

                  ⌒ Erin

I was in a great deal of pain caused by bed rest. My muscles
had atrophied and I felt very weak. I couldn't lift my four-
year-old son. Carrying a full laundry basket was tiring.
Almost every activity strained my back muscles. I joked with
friends that bed rest was the hardest thing I ever had to do
until I went vertical again.

                  ⌒ Kendra

According to a recent study, women who had been on bed rest resumed daily activity *at least* one week later than new mothers who had not been on bed rest, and they felt weak and out of shape for at least six weeks and often longer. Many mothers say they experienced bed rest's side effects for several months; some say for well over a year.

Overdoing it too soon and too quickly can complicate your recovery, too. "When you first get off bed rest, your muscles are very vulnerable to tears because the muscle fibers are weak and thin," says Dr. Maloni. She suggests taking those first steps slowly. Have someone assist you when you stand and walk. Move cautiously when you get up out of a chair, on and off the toilet, and up and down the stairs. Use a wheelchair or hold on to someone's arm when you visit your baby in the nursery.

Most importantly, ask your doctor to order a consultation with a physical therapist (PT) before leaving the hospital (or soon after). A PT can determine which muscles are most in need of rehabilitation and can then develop an individualized exercise program to help you recover. Also, check to see if your health insurance will cover home health care or a postpartum doula (someone who assists with child care, household work, and provides emotional support), especially if you're expecting to go home within a few days after delivery.

When you first start standing again, you may get dizzy or out of breath. This is because you're not at the same fitness level you were prior to bed rest: Your cardiovascular system has weakened. "Resuming activity after bed rest is like trying to go skiing after you've stopped for a few years," says Dr. Maloni. You'll need to begin vertical living slowly and take frequent rests.

Of course, telling you to take it slow is easier said than done. After sitting on the sidelines for so long, you're undoubtedly anxious to get back into the game. There's also a new baby who now needs you, too. And, after receiving so much household help, you're probably anxious to take over and give your partner and other helpers some much-deserved time off.

Many mothers become frustrated, even angry, when they cannot physically do all that they want right away. Keep in mind that you are recovering from two exhausting events: being on bed rest and having a baby. Try not to be too tough on yourself. Once again, you must ask for and accept help. As you regain your strength, you can slowly add more to your day and pay back the kindnesses of others.

The following tips from Cora Huitt, a physical therapist who has worked with pregnant women on bed rest for over ten years, can help you readjust to upright living.

To regain posture:

- Stand straight while keeping the top of your pelvis tilted and your bottom tucked under to lengthen your spine.

- Hold your head up and look straight.

- Bear your weight evenly on both feet.

- Gradually increase your standing tolerance by slowly increasing your activity level.

- Pull your stomach in to help support your back.

To resume daily activities:

- Bend with your legs instead of your waist to pick up items. (If your knees and leg muscles are quite weak, this may be difficult; consult your PT.)

- When working at the kitchen counter, slightly bend your knees to help keep your back straight, like a dancer. (This may be difficult if your knees are weak; consult your PT.)

- To carry your baby, laundry, or groceries, keep your elbows bent close to your sides, instead of straight.

- When vacuuming or sweeping, move your feet to stay close to the area you are cleaning.

To prevent back strain when sitting:

- Support your arms with pillows when reading or holding your baby.

- Use a footstool to help keep your bottom properly placed on your chair.

- Do not cross your legs.

GETTING YOUR BODY BACK

Stores and libraries are full of books and videos addressing how to get back into shape after pregnancy, but few address the special concerns of a woman who has endured weeks or months of inactivity. Though it is important for you to start a rehabilitation program soon after delivery, some exercises and movements can actually do more harm than good. Before you begin exercising, consult your doctor or PT. A prescription for a PT assessment, to determine which muscles are weak and need specific exercises for recovery, will help you avoid injury.

You should be able to do most of the simple exercises discussed in

The Aftereffects of Bed Rest

Women experience a number of symptoms following bed rest. In a recent study of eighty-nine women who had been on bed rest, over 50 percent said they experienced the following: back muscle soreness; difficulty walking, climbing, or descending stairs; low- or upper-leg muscle soreness; knee soreness and/or knee buckling; swelling in feet or legs; shortness of breath, dizziness, or feeling lightheaded; decreased appetite; fatigue; headache; trouble concentrating; mood changes; and depression. Other studies show additional emotional effects, such as frustration by the delay in resuming usual activities; difficulty concentrating; feeling overwhelmed; feelings of loss about the time spent on bed rest; and lack of energy. Physicians aren't always aware of bed rest's side effects, so tell your doctor about any symptoms you experience.

chapter 6, Couch Calisthenics, soon after delivery. But move slowly and carefully, progressing to more complex movements when you feel ready. A gradual program of abdominal and back exercises can help you regain muscle tone and strength, and a variety of activities will help your body resume its previous state. Walking and swimming are two activities commonly suggested for women following bed rest and delivery.

BLAST TO THE PAST

Resuming life after two months of hospital bed rest was like "returning from a very long trip," says Allison. "I was shocked that the world had gone on without me, and I had to adjust to all its changes."

Like Allison, many mothers describe the bed-rest experience with such phrases as "It felt like a time warp," or "It was like being in the twilight zone." The sense of time becomes distorted when you give up your everyday active life. Not leaving the hospital or the house can make the outside world seem foreign. You'll slowly need to take in the world that you've been removed from for so long. It may take you a while before you feel completely back to your usual social self.

After weeks of not leaving the hospital, re-entering the world was so bizarre. I checked into the hospital in the middle of April wearing a coat; I came out at the beginning of June wearing sandals. I missed a whole season. It felt odd that the rest of the world had gone on as usual, while my life had changed so much.

— Danielle

Since I hadn't been to stores or seen the outside world much during my bed rest, I had to walk slowly and take it all in when I first went out. My husband didn't understand this. He's a do-it-and-do-it-fast kind of guy. But I needed to take my time.

— Rachel

In addition, you may be confused by how you're feeling as you re-enter your old life. Though thrilled to be a part of the action again, you may be surprised to find yourself missing that alone time you had during bed rest. After holding everything together for so long, you may now need to let go, even cry a little. Unfortunately, few people may understand or want to talk about your conflicting feelings, and you may feel guilty about complaining.

I guess everyone figured I was fine after about a month after my baby's birth. But I wasn't fine. I was still very sick, in pain, and weak. I had a newborn baby, a preemie to boot, and a twenty-one-month-old to take care of. I was still trying to deal with my near-death experience and a hysterectomy. I found it hard to talk about things because everyone wanted to be so positive about the birth and my health.

— Jackie

Keep in mind that you're making other adjustments in your life, too. If you're a first-time mom, you're adapting to new motherhood. If you have other children, you're focusing some of your attention on helping siblings adjust to a new baby. There is added stress if you have multiples or a preemie, or preemie multiples, or one or more of your babies died.

Just as bed rest affects you physically, it has impacted you in many other ways. You are no longer the same person you were prior to bed rest. You'll need to adjust to and reflect on these changes, and friends and family may need time to get accustomed to the new you.

> *My high-risk pregnancy and bed rest put my life into perspective. I almost lost my baby and I almost died during delivery. Suddenly, things that once seemed important—going out with friends, having money, taking trips—no longer were. What matters most to me now is my family and our health. I guess this is one good thing that came out of my bed rest—besides my baby!*
>
> — Allison

ADJUSTING TO DAILY LIVING

> *Even grocery shopping took me over an hour because I couldn't stay focused on the task at hand.*
>
> — Allison

If you find it hard to drive your car, shop, or eat in a crowded restaurant after bed rest, you're not alone. For many women, the sights and sounds they were deprived of during bed rest become difficult to handle afterward. "Bed rest is a type of sensory deprivation," says Dr. Maloni. "When you first start going back out, you feel overloaded because you aren't used to all that stimulation."

Going out was exhausting. Things were too bright, too fast, and too loud. Some part of me was glad to be out and about while another part wanted nothing more than to get home and be safe.

⌒ Teri

When the baby was about a month old, I took my toddler to a play group at a neighbor's house. As soon as I got there, I couldn't wait to go home! It was so loud—all those kids running about. The moms were really loud, too. I swear somebody must have spiked the orange juice they were drinking, because nobody could be that loud at eleven o'clock in the morning.

⌒ Rachel

I was released from bed rest the day before Labor Day so I was able to go to our Labor Day community picnic. I hungered for conversation, but I felt so lost. I had been so focused on pregnancy and bed rest that I didn't feel I could just chat anymore. I felt like I was out of practice with my social skills.

⌒ Erin

Just as you must allow your body to heal following a high-risk pregnancy and bed rest, you also need to let your mind heal. If going out becomes too overwhelming, shorten your excursions. Take in the world a little at a time. When you become tired, rest or take a nap. The stress-reducing techniques discussed in chapter 9 can also help. Experts say it can take months, even as long as a year, for a woman to feel like her old self again.

PUTTING BED REST BEHIND YOU

Some experts say women who experienced major stress during pregnancy and problems during delivery are at increased risk for mood disorders after delivery. Mood disorders can range from feeling blue (70 percent of new mothers do within a few weeks of their baby's homecoming) to more serious depression (about 10 to 15 percent of mothers experience depression before their baby's first birthday). If you suffered a loss or delivered prematurely, you are also at greater risk.

Consult your doctor or a qualified therapist if one or more of the following symptoms last longer than a week: difficulty sleeping (getting to sleep or frequently waking up); feeling guilty, helpless, or hopeless much of the time; a decreased appetite; a significant weight loss or gain; feeling unloved or rejected; difficulty concentrating or thinking; lack of interest in your baby or yourself; panic attacks; a decreased interest in usual activities; and/or persistent thoughts of death or violence.

If left untreated, depression can threaten your (and your baby's) health and safety. Do not feel weak if you need help dealing with your feelings. Recognizing when help is needed takes strength, and is one of the best things you can do for yourself—and for your baby.

If you're feeling sad and you haven't already connected with a bed-rest support network, now is a good time to do so (see Bed Rest/Support in appendix D; E-mail lists focusing on life after bed rest can be found at many large parenting Web sites). Talking with others who understand bed-rest recovery and listening to their experiences can be a great source of comfort. A bed-rest veteran may be the only person who truly understands how you're feeling.

On a personal note, it's been over eight years since my last bed rest, so I was truly surprised by my emotions as I began talking with other bed-rest veterans in preparation for this book. Once my children were born, I figured I should "get over it" and enjoy my babies. I never allowed myself to grieve over the losses caused by my problem pregnancies, and I buried those feelings. Thanks to the support of the Bed Rest Book Buddies and the other women and men who shared their stories, I've now come to terms with my not-so-perfect pregnancies.

I hope your healing following bed rest comes much easier and earlier for you. We're all unique individuals, and we each cope differently with life's challenges. Once you've accepted bed rest, you may embrace it as an opportunity for personal growth. Or, it may take you many years to view bed rest as a positive influence in your life, if you ever do.

I now appreciate my bed-rest experiences for what they gave me:

strength, humility, friendships, and a purpose in life to help other women through my writing. Bed rest also gave me an incredible appreciation for my family; not a day goes by when I don't count my blessings. These are valuable lessons, ones that can take others a lifetime to learn.

WHO CAN HELP

Also see Who Can Help in chapters 7 and 9.

Depression After Delivery
P.O. Box 278
Belle Mead, NJ 08502
(800) 944-4PPD ((800) 944-4773)
www.depressionafterdelivery.com

Doulas of North America
13513 N. Grove Drive
Alpine, UT 84004
(801) 756-7331
www.dona.com

Postpartum Education for Parents:
www.sbpep.org

Postpartum Support International
927 N. Kellogg Ave.

Santa Barbara, CA 93111

(805) 967-7636

www.postpartum.net

Recommended Reading

Also see Recommended Reading in chapters 6 and 9.

Overcoming Postpartum Depression and Anxiety by Linda Sebastian (Addicus Books, 1998)

This Isn't What I Expected: Overcoming Postpartum Depression by Karen R. Kleiman, M.S.W., and Valerie D. Raskin, M.D. (Bantam Books, 1994)

Suggested Video

BabyJoy: Exercises and Activities for Parents and Newborns, Elizabeth Noble, P.T., and Leo Sorger, M.D. (New Life Images); www.elizabethnoble.com

Your Bed Rest Checklist

My doctor prescribes:

_____ Reduced activity and frequent periods of lying down (I should lie down after _____ hours of activity for at least _____ minutes/hours)

_____ Very little activity, mostly lying down (I should lie down after _____ minutes of activity for at least _____ hours)

_____ Bed rest at home with bathroom privileges

_____ Bed rest at home with no bathroom privileges

_____ Hospitalization without strict bed rest

_____ Hospitalization with bathroom privileges

_____ Hospitalization with no bathroom privileges

I can expect to be on bed rest for:

____ (days/weeks/months) (your doctor may not be able to answer this)

My doctor recommends the following bed-rest position: _____
_____

_____

_____

_____

_____

Job

I can:

____ Continue working at my job

____ Work part time

____ Work at home sitting up for _____ hours a day

____ Work at home lying down for _____ hours a day

Bathroom Privileges

I can:

____ Use the bathroom (if you're experiencing preterm labor, it's important to keep your bladder empty)

____ Use a bedpan

_____ Use a catheter

_____ Shower/bathe every day for about _____ minutes

_____ Shower/bathe every _____ days for about _____ minutes

Meals

I can eat:

_____ At the dinner table

_____ Sitting up in bed

_____ Lying down

Driving

I can:

_____ Drive my car for short distances

_____ Be a passenger sitting

_____ Be a passenger lying down in the backseat

_____ Drive to medical appointments only

_____ Be a passenger on the way to medical appointments (sitting up/lying down)

Home

I can:

_____ Do housework (dusting, cleaning bathrooms, laundry) for _____ minutes a day

_____ Do light housework (loading dishwasher, easy cooking) for _____ minutes a day

_____ Shop for _____ minutes each week

I shouldn't lift anything larger than _____ or heavier than

_____

Children

I can:

_____ Take care of my children

_____ Lift my children

_____ Bathe my children

Intimacy

I can:

_____ Engage in sexual intercourse

_____ Engage in sexual acts that cause orgasm

_____ Engage in sexual acts that cause arousal and stimulation (for example, nipple stimulation)

Activity Changes

I can increase activity if: _____

_____

_____

_____

_____

_____

I should decrease activity if: _____

_____

_____

_____

_____

_____

I should call my doctor immediately if (also refer to appendix C): _____

_____

_____

_____

_____

_____

Prescribed Medications: _____

_____

Notes:

Names, Numbers, and Notes

Partner

Office: _____

Cellular phone: _____

Pager: _____

Health Care

In case of an emergency, call: _____

My doctor: _____ Phone: _____

Perinatologist: _____ Phone: _____

Backup physician(s): _____ Phone: _____

_____ Phone: _____

_____ Phone: _____

Nurse(s): _____ Phone: _____

_____ Phone: _____

If after hours, call:_____

Hospital: _____ _____

Health insurance: _____ _____

Pharmacist: _____ Phone: _____

Physical therapist: _____ Phone: _____

Occupational therapist: _____ Phone: _____

Dietitian: _____ Phone: _____

Home health-care aide(s): _____ Phone: _____

_____ Phone: _____

_____ Phone: _____

Friends, Family, and Neighbors

_____ Phone: _____

_____ Phone: _____

_____ Phone: _____

_____ Phone: _____

_____ Phone: _____

Job

Employer: _____ Phone: _____

Coworker(s): _____ Phone: _____

_____ Phone: _____

_____ Phone: _____

Human resources: _____ Phone: _____

_____ Phone: _____

Child Care

Child care/school(s):

_____ Phone: _____

_____ Phone: _____

Baby-sitter(s)_____ Phone: _____

_____ Phone: _____

_____ Phone: _____

Mother's helpers:_____ Phone: _____

_____ Phone: _____

_____ Phone: _____

Car-pool contacts: _____ Phone: _____

_____ Phone: _____

_____ Phone: _____

Children's friends: _____ Phone: _____

_____ Phone: _____

_____ Phone: _____

_____ Phone: _____

Household

Bank: _____ Phone: _____

Electrician _____ Phone: _____

Plumber: _____ Phone: _____

Home repairs: _____ Phone: _____

Dry cleaner:_____ Phone: _____

Laundry service: _____ Phone: _____

Meals

Food delivery: _____ Phone: _____

_____ Phone: _____

_____ Phone: _____

_____ Phone: _____

Grocery delivery: _____ Phone: _____

_____ Phone: _____

_____ Phone: _____

Entertainment

Library: _____ Web site: _____

Video store: _____ Phone: _____

Bookstore: _____ Phone: _____

Craft supply store: _____ Phone: _____

Bed-Rest Support

Sidelines National Support Group: (949) 497-2265; www.sidelines.org

Local Sidelines chapter: _____

Contact(s): _____ Phone: _____

_____ Phone: _____

_____ Phone: _____

_____ Phone: _____

Local or hospital support group: _____

Contact(s): _____ Phone: _____

_____ Phone: _____

_____ Phone: _____

Bed-Rest Web sites and mailing lists:

www.pregnancybedrest.com

_____

_____

_____

People/organizations who have offered to help:

_____ Phone: _____

_____ Phone: _____

_____ Phone: _____

_____ Phone: _____

Notes: _____

_____

_____

_____

_____

_____

_____

_____

_____

When to Call Your Doctor

Do not hesitate to call your doctor if you experience any of these symptoms:

- *Uterine contractions that are fifteen minutes apart or closer.* Your abdomen feels tight or hard, four or more times an hour. You may or may not feel pain.

- *Menstrual-like cramps.* Cramps are above the public bone. They may be constant or come and go.

- *Low, dull backache.* Pain may be constant or come and go. Changing position does not relieve discomfort.

- *Pelvic pressure.* You may feel heavy in front, like the baby is pushing down on your pelvis.

- *Increase or change in vaginal discharge.* You experience more than the usual amount and/or discharge becomes more mucus-like or watery, or the color becomes more pink or bloody.

- *Fluid leaks from the vagina.*

- *Abdominal cramping.* May feel like bad gas pains, with or without diarrhea.

More Helpful Resources and Reading

Resources and recommended reading related to chapter topics are listed at the end of most chapters. Additional organizations, Web sites, and reading material are listed below. For recent updates or to recommend a listing, please visit www.pregnancybedrest.com, or write:

Amy E. Tracy
445C E. Cheyenne Mountain Blvd.
P.M.B. 194
Colorado Springs, CO 80906

ADVOCACY GROUPS

Coalition for Positive Outcomes in Pregnancy
507 Capital Court, N.E.
Washington, DC 20002

(202) 544-7499

www.storknet.org/CPOP/

Coalition for Prematurity Awareness

P.O. Box 9667

Wyoming, MI 49509

(616) 534-9146

www.preemieawareness.org

BED REST

Support

The Confinement Line

c/o The Childbirth Education Association

P.O. Box 1609

Springfield, VA 22151

(703) 941-7183

Mothers of Supertwins (MOST)

P.O. Box 951

Brentwood, NY 11717

(631) 859-1110

www.mostonline.org

Sidelines National Support Network

P.O. Box 1808

Laguna Beach, CA 92652

(949) 497-2265

www.sidelines.org

The Triplet Connection

P.O. Box 99571

Stockton, CA 95209

(209) 474-0885

www.tripletconnection.org

Publications

"Antepartum Bed Rest: Case Studies, Research, and Nursing Care" by Judith A. Maloni, Ph.D., R.N., 1998. Available from: Association of Women's Health, Obstetric and Neonatal Nurses, 2000 L St., N.W., Suite 740, Washington, DC 20036; (800) 673-8499; www.awhonn.org

Bedrest Before Baby: What's a Mother to Do? by Patricia D. Isennock, R.N., M.S. (Mustard Seed Publications, 1992) (out of print; check your library or used bookstore)

The Bed Rest Survival Guide by Barbara Edelston Peterson (Avon, 1998)

"Coping with Bedrest in Pregnancy" by Jamie Eloise Bolane and Jane Furlong, 1994. Available from: Childbirth Graphics, P.O.

Box 21207, Waco, TX 76702; (800) 299-3366;
www.childbirthgraphics.com

Days in Waiting: A Guide to Surviving Pregnancy Bedrest by Mary
Ann McCann (deRuyter-Nelson, 1999)

Pregnancy Bedrest: A Guide for the Pregnant Woman and Her Family by
Susan H. Johnston, M.S.W., and Deborah A. Kraut, M.I.L.R. (Henry
Holt, 1990) (out of print; check your library or used bookstore)

E-mail Lists

The Bed Rest Book Buddies: www.pregnancybedrest.com
Sidelines: www.sidelines.org/chat3.htm

Also look for lists at:
www.americanbaby.com
www.babycenter.com
www.childbirth.org
www.clubmom.com
www.iParenting.com
www.momsonline.com
www.parenthoodweb.com
www.parentsoup.com
www.parentsplace.com
www.thelaboroflove.com

Web Sites

Bed Rest in Multiple Pregnancy:
http://multiples.about.com/parenting/multiples/library/blbedrst.htm
www.twinslist.org/bedrest.htm

Moms on Bed Rest:
www.momsonbedrest.com

Pregnancy Bed Rest:
www.pregnancybedrest.com

Pregnancy Bed Rest Web (Dr. Judith Maloni's site):
http://armstrong.son.wisc.edu/~son/bedrest/

BEREAVEMENT

Bereavement Services
Gunderson Lutheran Medical Center
1910 South Ave.
La Crosse, WI 54601
(800) 362-9567 (ext. 4747)
www.gundluth.org/bereave

Center for Loss in Multiple Birth
P.O. Box 91377
Anchorage, AK 99509

(907) 222-5321

www.climb-support.org

Centering Corporation

1531 N. Saddle Creek Road

Omaha, NE 68104

(402) 553-1200

www.centering.org

Compassionate Friends

P.O. Box 3696

Oak Brook, IL 60522

(877) 969-0010

www.compassionatefriends.org

A Place to Remember

1885 University Ave., Suite 110

St. Paul, MN 55104

(800) 631-0973

www.aplacetoremember.com

SHARE Pregnancy and Infant Loss Support

St. Joseph Health Center

300 First Capitol Drive

St. Charles, MO 63301

(800) 821-6819

www.nationalshareoffice.com

Publications

"The Bereavement Kit." Available from: March of Dimes Resource Center, 1275 Mamaroneck Ave., White Plains, NY 10605; (888) MODIMES ((888) 663-4637); www.modimes.org

Empty Cradle, Broken Heart by Deborah L. Davis, Ph.D. (Fulcrum, 1999)

Pregnancy After a Loss: A Guide to Pregnancy After a Miscarriage, Stillbirth, or Infant Death by Carol Cirulli Lanham (Berkley, 1999); www.pregnancyafteraloss.com

A Silent Sorrow: Pregnancy Loss, 2nd ed., by Ingrid Kohn, et al. (Routledge, 2000)

Web Sites

Resources for bereaved families:
www.hygeia.org
www.misschildren.org

COMPLICATIONS IN PREGNANCY

Also see Recommended Reading in chapter 1.

March of Dimes Resource Center
1275 Mamaroneck Ave.
White Plains, NY 10605
888-MODIMES ((888) 663-4637)
(800) 367-6630 (product catalogue)
www.modimes.org

Asthma

American Lung Association
1740 Broadway
New York, NY 10019
(800) LUNG USA ((800) 586-4872)
www.lungusa.org

Gestational Diabetes

American Diabetes Association
1701 N. Beauregard St.
Alexandria, VA 22311
(800) DIABETES ((800) 342-2383)
www.diabetes.org

Gestational Diabetes: What to Expect, 4th ed. (NTC/Contemporary Publishing, 2001)

Managing Your Gestational Diabetes by Lois Jovanovic-Peterson, M.D. (Chronimed Publishing, 1998)

Understanding Gestational Diabetes: A Practical Guide to a Healthy Pregnancy, 2000. Available from: National Institute of Child Health and Human Development, 31 Center Drive, Building 31, Room 2A32, M.S.C. 2425, Bethesda, MD 20892; (800) 370-2943; www.nichd.nih.gov (search "gestational diabetes")

Group B Strep

Group B Strep Association
P.O. Box 16515
Chapel Hill, NC 27516
(919) 932-5344
www.groupbstrep.org

HELLP Syndrome

HELLP Syndrome Society
P.O. Box 44
Bethany, WV 26032
http://hometown.aol.com/hellp1995/hellp.html

High Blood Pressure

Blood pressure:
www.bloodpressure.com

Hypertension in pregnancy:
http://pregnancy.about.com/health/pregnancy/library/weekly/aa102
   698.htm

Incompetent Cervix

IC and pregnancy:
www.geocities.com/incompetentcervix/

Preeclampsia

Preeclampsia Foundation
P.O. Box 52993
Bellevue, WA 98015
(800) 665-9341
www.preeclampsia.org

Premature Rupture of Membranes

The PROM Page and PROM Forum:
www.kanalen.org/prom/

Preterm Labor

Every Pregnant Woman's Guide to Preventing Premature Birth by
Barbara Luke (Random House, 1995) (out of print; check your
library or used bookstore)

*The Premature Labor Handbook: Successfully Sustaining Your High-
Risk Pregnancy* by Patricia Anne Robertson, M.D., and Peggy
Henning Berlin, Ph.D. (Doubleday, 1986) (out of print; check
your library or used bookstore)

Preterm labor management audiocassette:
(864) 244-4331
www.newwaychildbirth.com

Preventing Preterm Birth: A Parent's Guide by Michael Katz, M.D.,
Pamela Gill, R.N., M.S.N, and Judith Turiel, Ed.D. (Health
Publishing Co., 1988) (out of print; check your library or used
bookstore)

Twin-to-Twin Transfusion

Twin Hope
2592 W. 14th St.
Cleveland, OH 44113
(440) 353-1933
www.twinhope.com

Twin to Twin Transfusion Syndrome Foundation
411 Longbeach Parkway
Bay Village, OH 44140
(216) 899-TTTS ((216) 899-8887)
www.tttsfoundation.org

HEALTH WEB SITES

Health Answers:
www.healthanswers.com

Health Finder:
www.healthfinder.com

Intelihealth:
www.intelihealth.com

Medscape:
www.medscape.com

National Institutes of Health:
www.nih.gov/health

National Women's Health Resource Center:
www.healthywomen.org

WebMD:
www.webmd.com

Multiples

Also see Bed Rest/Support.

National Organization of Mothers of Twins Clubs
P.O. Box 438
Thompson Station, TN 37179
(877) 540-2200
www.nomotc.org

Parents of Multiple Births Association of Canada
P.O. Box 234
Gormley, Ontario, Canada L0H 1G0
(905) 888-0725
www.pomba.org

Twin Services
3941C Darien Highway
Brunswick, GA 31525
(912) 267-1452
www.twinservices.com

TwInsight
1137 Second St., Suite 109
Santa Monica, CA 90403
(310) 458-1373
www.twinsight.com

Publications

The Art of Parenting Twins by Patricia Maxwell Malmstrom and
Janet Poland (Ballantine, 1999)

Everything You Need to Know to Have a Healthy Twin Pregnancy by
Gila Leiter, M.D. (Dell, 2000)

Having Twins, 3rd ed., by Elizabeth Noble (Houghton Mifflin,
1991)

Raising Twins by Eileen M. Pearlman, Ph.D., and Jill Alison Ganon
(HarperCollins, 2000)

Twins Magazine, 5350 S. Roslyn St., Suite 400, Englewood, CO
80111; (888) 55-TWINS ((888) 558-9467);
www.twinsmagazine.com

Twins! Pregnancy, Birth and the First Year of Life by Connie L.
Agnew, M.D., Alan H. Klein, M.D., and Jill Alison Ganon
(HarperCollins, 1997)

When You're Expecting Twins, Triplets, or Quads by Barbara Luke,
M.D., and Tamara Eberlein (HarperCollins, 1999)

Web Sites

Multiplicity:
www.geocities.com/synspectrum/multiplicity.html
Twins List:
www.twinslist.org

PREMATURE BIRTH

Also see Advocacy Groups.

The Alexis Foundation for Premature Infants and Children
P.O. Box 1126
Birmingham, MI 48012
(877) ALEXIS-0 ((877) 253-9470)
http://pages.prodigy.net/thealexisfoundation/THEALEXIS1.html

For a complete list of resources for preemie parents, visit:
www.preemieparents.com

Publications

The Emotional Journey of Parenting Your Premature Baby: A Book of Hope and Healing by Deborah Davis, Ph.D., and Mara Tesler Stein, Psy.D. (NICU Ink; 2002); www.preemieparentsupport.com

Your Premature Baby and Child: Helpful Answers and Advice for Parents by Amy E. Tracy and Dianne I. Maroney (Berkley, 1999); www.preemieparents.com

E-mail Lists

Early Blessings:
http://earlyblessings.homestead.com/EB1.html

Parents of Premature Babies:

www.preemie-l.org

The Preemie Place:

www.thepreemieplace.com

Preemies Organization:

www.preemies.org

Premature Child:

www.comeunity.com/premature/preemielists.html

SINGLE MOTHERS

Parents Without Partners

1650 S. Dixie Highway, Suite 510

Boca Raton, FL 33432

(561) 391-8833

www.parentswithoutpartners.org

TEEN MOTHERS

For Teen Moms Only

P.O. Box 962

Frankfort, IL 60423

(815) 464-5465

www.forteenmomsonly.com

INDEX